CONCILIUM

Religion in the Eighties

CONCILIUM

Concilium 140 (10/1980): Moral Theology

CHRISTIAN ETHICS AND ECONOMICS: THE NORTH-SOUTH CONFLICT

Edited by

Dietmar Mieth

and

Jacques Pohier

English Language Editor
Marcus Lefébure

T. & T. CLARK LTD.
Edinburgh

THE SEABURY PRESS
New York

December 1980
T. & T. Clark Ltd., 36 George Street, Edinburgh EH2 2LQ
ISBN: 0 567 30020 X

The Seabury Press, 815 Second Avenue, New York, N.Y. 10017
ISBN: 0 8164 2282 6

Library of Congress Catalog Card No.: 80 50892

Printed in Scotland by William Blackwood & Sons Ltd., Edinburgh

Concilium: Monthly except July and August.
Subscriptions 1981: All countries (except U.S.A. and Canada) £27·00 postage and handling included; U.S.A. and Canada $64.00 postage and handling included. (Second class postage licence 541-530 at New York, N.Y.) Subscription distribution in U.S. by Expediters of the Printed Word Ltd., 527 Madison Avenue, Suite 1217, New York, N.Y. 10022.

CONTENTS

Part III
Attempts at a Christian Response

Editorial

THE PRESENT issue of *Concilium* is devoted in the first place to the ethical aspects of international economic problems. Both the theme of Ethics and Economics and the paradigm of the North-South conflict are the subject of a great deal of ideological controversy. This is why the way in which we should deal with this issue was very thoroughly discussed. Unfortunately we could not see this right the way through. This is the reason why, for instance, an article about various Marxist approaches to development policy (and their own crises!) did not come off. There were fewer authors from the Third World than we had envisaged. All that we could do was to begin to define the Christian-ethical priorities in respect of individual economic factors. What we came to realise was that in the future we should have to single out any one such factor as the subject-matter of the whole issue. The corresponding issue devoted to moral theology in 1982 will, therefore, concern itself with the problems of international unemployment.

This issue of *Concilium* therefore represents a preliminary balance-sheet of the problems. Its three parts are given over to an analysis of the economic factors, of the general political and economic theories about the North-South conflict and, finally, of the potential for ethical reflection in the Christian context and the way in which this determines the direction and commitment of Christian and Church practice. Our hope is that this balance-sheet will provoke further discussion and research. For this issue is undoubtedly stronger in the raising of problems than in their soluiton.

1. SURVEY OF THE CONTENTS

The individual articles on the economic factors in the North-South conflict (population, energy and food policies; world trade system; financial policy; multinational companies and technology) establish the following areas of reference:

Paul *Steidl-Meier* sees injustice to consist above all in maldistribution. It is only to the extent that political responsibility comes to embody the principles of just distribution that it will be possible to ensure a better sharing of energy—and also food resources, changes in the methods of production and technology and the requisite structural changes in society. This contribution also comprises a methodological reflection on the relationship between facts and values and a consideration of the application of the principles of the Church's social teaching (which should be compared with the articles by Chenu, Wogaman and Lucal).

Siro *Lombardini* describes the typology of the structural exploitation of the countries of the Third World on account of the capitalist structure of world trade. The necessity of trade becomes in this way evident, although the author is reserved about an ethically-based politico-economic strategy (in contrast to the authors of the articles on theories of dependence).

Hanns *Abele* demonstrates the relationship between the regulation of finance in the prevailing economic order and the progressive indebtedness of the developing countries. The different interests which the industrialised nations (as creditors) and the developing nations (as debtors) have in relation to each other reinforce the problem. What the economist is saying is that a resolution is a matter not of merely technical contrivance but of ethics and in particular of just distribution.

Roger *Riddell* concerns himself with the economic and technological monopolies of transnational corporations and their effects on the ever-worsening imbalance. The production of goods, the system of employment and even national sovereignty are caught up in this process. Only a strict control of the policy of such corporations and their derivations offers any hope of regulating poverty and unemployment. A more equitable international distribution is not feasible as long as the policy of growth is not redirected.

However various these contributions are, they do converge unambiguously on the economically and ethically based demand for a change in politico-economic strategies on a world level and on the consciousness that the political will must be guided by ethical priorities.

The relationship between economics, politics and ethical responsibility is then discussed in a general manner in relationship to theories of the North-South conflict. This is what the articles in the second part deal with. They address themselves to the previously identified obstacles to distributive justice in the form of political will and the consequential economic factors:

Vincent *Cosmao* demonstrates the blocking effect of a political ideology of national security. (Whilst these very lines were being penned, it was possible to observe its tendency to work anti-democratically in Bolivia.) The ideology of security as a condition for freedom (for the few!) seeks to justify itself as Christian. To this end it makes use of the integration of 'Christendom' into the industrial system and of the familiar bogy of the communist enemy of Christendom. The counterpart of this is to set about a reflection on the political function of Christian belief which renounces the sacralisation of any particular political order (*a propos* of which a comparison with Dussel's analysis of the Puebla Document at the end of this issue is instructive).

It is as much out of the question to allow political stability to take absolute priority over the removal of social injustice as it is to allow the twin systematic factors of the market economy (supply and demand) to bring about on their own the removal of the unjust distribution in the world economy. Pieter *Verloren van Themaat* describes the new world economic order as a 'mixed economic order' which needs conscious intervention to supplement the laws of the market. The development of multilateral treaties, the establishment of economic rights and duties between States and supranational obligations in solidarity are more and more recognised to be in the economic self-interest of countries, and therein lies the chance of their realisation.

Before that can happen, however, the norms of economic inter-dependence are blocked by the facts of one-sided dependence. The following articles therefore concern themselves with the so-called 'theory of dependence' and the ensuing strategic considerations about a partial dissociation and 'self-reliance' on the part of the developing countries. Georges *Enderle* and Ambros *Lüthi* restrict themselves to analysis stemming from the Latin-American sub-continent. Here political, sociological and economic factors are bound together into one theory. Historical experiences show the disadvantages of models of development which through their orientation to industrial centres have reinforced or exacerbated the relationship of dependence. In this perspective the economic and technological dependence appears to be less of a transitional catalyst of self-development and more of a hindrance. The essential defect seems to consist in the fact that the self-propelling development of the industrialised countries has not reproduced itself in the countries of the Third World. In this way the aims of growth in productivity and reduction of inequality diverge from each other. The strategic conclusion to effect a total or partial dissociation therefore serves the aim of 'introducing the mass of men to productive employment and to satisfy their basic needs'. Dieter *Senghaas's* article shows us the historical origin of this way of looking at the problem; he seeks to combine a case for the selective and temporary dissociation from the tradition of the market economy with the long-term interests of the industrialised countries.

In the face of a certain convergence of these theoretical reflections on development (which should be read in the light of the change in the images of pragmatic development aid described by John Lucal in his article), the ethician poses the question: If the aim of distributive justice is clear, how is it that the strategic means come to be ideologically differentiated? That this problem is not yet resolved emerges from the attempts to provide Christian-ethical answers, the upshot of which (without any claim to comprehensiveness) appears in the third part.

In the foreground we find the evangelical protest against exploitation and violence, that is to say, against poverty and dependence. This articulates itself in terms of concrete demands for the satisfaction of basic material needs, human rights, equality of opportunity and the facilitation of a sharing society. The power that Christian faith has to motivate the formulation of ethical aims (Wogaman) is prolonged into pragmatic commitment (Lucal) and is sharpened up in the praxis of liberation theology (Gutierrez and Dussel). This is to make an opposition between a 'development' from 'outside' and 'on top' and an unfolding of the base 'from below'. What then becomes obvious is that there is still a yawning gap between the problems of macro-economic aims and strategies and a Christian-inspired work at the grass-roots. One gets the impression that the ethics of economics is concerned with the overall direction of distribution from above and thereby takes only an extrinsic and an insufficiently explicit cognisance of the concrete problems of power relationships. We shall come back to this problem.

Hans *Schöpfer* then makes a plea for a more theological responsibility, taking as his point of departure the Report of the Brandt Commission, and after that Marie-Dominique *Chenu* tackles the problem of the role of the Church's social teaching. In this regard he discerns a shift of paradigm since Vatican II. He makes a distinction between a closed social doctrine of the Church and the new concept of a theologically ethical information and guidance of social analyses, the formulation of socio-economic objectives and trade strategies. The closed social doctrine of the Church is open to the objection that it proceeded from a 'deist' notion of God and from statically and quasi-cosmologically essentialist conceptions of society.

It therefore got tied up with socio-cultural categories defined in historical and geographical terms. It was used in the service of the triumphalist enterprise of grounding a specifically Christian 'third way' between capitalism and socialism, applicable in a deductive way to any situation, irrespective of a historical analysis. And finally the stress was far more on the docility of obedient Christians than on their creativity. This doctrine has in the meantime been quietly abandoned, above all in the declarations of the last popes, even if this had unfortunately gone unnoticed by their highly-placed interpreters in the industrialised countries. What now stands out is no longer the unity of utterances but their suitability to situations and their human relevance, without this involving the abandonment of the most important social principles. What this amounts to is bringing out the evangelical potential of various social philosophies, so that one does not exhaust oneself in making an apologia for one's own doctrine, which has in any case shown itself to be capable of abuse.

John Philip *Wogaman* seeks to bring together the evangelical impulse and ethical reflection in a methodological article. The ethical character of situations of changing interests can be extracted to the extent that ethical values are related to their transcendent source. It is the 'ultimate nature of reality'—which we glimpse only in part but which we grasp in faith—that bestows 'ethical significance' on economic life. The ethical method in the Christian context consists in drawing out the implications of the economic determinants in the light of this sense rationally. The ethical priority can then accord with other ethical elements.

A paradigm has also taken place in the practical work of Church development aid, as John *Lucal* shows. There has been a progression from the image of caritative help, through the model of economic development, to the image of a change of social structure which alone can make a fairer distribution possible. Because unjust social and political structures are the main obstacles, justice is more important than charity. The transition from this awareness to practice is taking place rather slowly, and especially amongst the organs of Church development work in the First World. This is due to the fact that consciousness of giving charitable help is more satisfying for the agents thereof than working for what is due. There is, however, also the problem of the politicisation of development as a result of thinking of it in terms of changing the structures. John Lucal's response to this is to say that if the Church in its work for development is to see the ideological problems that are tied up with it practically, then it must strengthen its social commitment in a pragmatic manner and thereby test the ideological influences critically. Above all the Church herself needs to change so that it corresponds inwardly and outwardly with the concept of solidarity.

The note of involvement is to be observed in all these authors, but it takes on a quite new resonance in the articles about liberation theology. Reflection and the witness of practical experience are here inseparable.

Gustavo *Guttierrez* describes the total contradiction between the institutionalised misuse of power and man's authentic right to life. What is in question here is not the awareness of the right principles and effective judgments about priorities but the unworkability of ethical maxims which are clearly recognisable in the context of faith. This is the situation of 'social sin'. The history of the 'Christianising' of South America has taken place under the sign of the death myth involved in the search for gold rather than as a matter of manifesting the contradiction of the message of the kingdom of God. It is not the aims of structural change which are unclear but who is to bring them about. Gutierrez here sees a new possibility in the Christian basic communities. They are the carriers of a new ethic of discipleship that rests upon the evangelical dialectic of grace and moral demand. Its power is shown in martyrdom (Archbishop Romero) and thereby unmasks the false option for death.

The thesis that Enrique *Dussel* expounds in his analysis of the final documents of Puebla runs as follows: the Christian ethic, with its central maxims about the priority of the liberation of the disadvantaged over any self-realisation, finds its primary expression in the economy. Christian ethics become real and effective only where economic relationships promote the communicative, and not merely the material and consumerist, productivity of human work. Through this analysis of the documents Dussel underlines the main points brought out by Gutierrez ('social sin', 'option for the poor').

2. CONVERGENCES AND DIVERGENCES OF AN ETHICAL BALANCE-SHEET

The inequitable distribution of economic goods as we come to experience the limits of growth is the most important concrete ethical problem of our time. Its urgency is manifest in all the articles. What also emerges is how economic and political injustice are inseparable. As with all concrete ethical problems it is, however, much easier to agree about the experience of contrast and the corresponding protest than about the ethical priorities and the strategic norms. At the same time it is also clear from all the articles that the Christian context of ethical reflection does not make for any softening of the problem. It also comes out that there is a large measure of consensus about the aims and the ethical principles. The overriding aim is the right to social *sharing*, and in the face of the hegemony of the economic right to *exchange* as the criterion of international economic relationships, this is no self-evidence. The right to share is based on the principle of the equality of all men and not on the equality of economically powerful subjects. Since it is not only concerned with material goods but includes man's rights, it also entails the principles of free self-administration and solidarity. The problem that arises in particular instances is how to do justice to these principles as a whole amidst the pressures of practical life, and this is not least a problem of political ethics. An ethic of economics that is not in the service of a political ethic is defective.

Distributive justice therefore presupposes an inhibition of the economic and political factors that block it and a facilitation of the structures that promote it. It therefore starts from the reality that is defective and seeks to take the possible steps that could improve things. In this way all ethical deductions from principles take on a practical and inductive aspect. The greater the commitment and the practical involvement, the more important this aspect will become. An ethic of some 'neutral' observer, which is still the one that prevails in our tradition and is traceable in many articles, thereby becomes more or less out of the question. Herein lies the conflict between the tradition of philosophical ethics and the ethos of liberation theologies which start from the evangelical conviction that taking the side of the disadvantaged is the only ethical stance they can expect. This is where we can detect the divergence between 'analytical' ethics and the ethos of committed Christians. The former see the main problem to consist in making an exact analysis of the conflict of aims and means and shy away from the ideological predisposition of those who maintain that securing a just society is above all a matter of the historical diagnosis of evil and of a wholehearted effort to overcome it. The latter see the ideological danger of an 'ideology of ideologylessness', the very technical expertise in defining the problems of ethical behaviour of which serves as a practical block and thereby preserves the existing injustice.

All that we wish to do here is to bring out into the open rather than study this problem which deserves to be dealt with thoroughly in Christian fundamental ethics. And what does emerge from a balance-sheet of the individual articles of this issue is an interesting convergence between analytical effort and committed orthopraxis precisely in regard to distributive justice: according to John Rawls (the final section of Philip Wogaman's article is interesting in this regard) the most disadvantaged is the subject of ethical decision, however much inequality in actual purchasing power may have to be tolerated, and it consists in working for the progressive removal of this disadvantage. According to liberation theologians who take their stand on orthopraxis it is the poor who are the 'subject' of the praxis of solidarity which brings about justice. This means that there is at least agreement about the strategic norm for distributive justice: the deterioration of relationships between North and South, with its horrific implications of the pauperisation and annhilation of a great part of mankind, cannot in the last analysis be reversed either through selective sharing in the economic growth of the industrialised and oil-producing countries or through internation guarantees of more equitable exchange. No, it is rather that every politico-economic decision is so charged with ethical responsibility that the broad 'base' of the disadvantaged peoples of the Third World cannot agree to it.

The diagnosis is clearly to the effect that the application of this strategic norm is blocked by economic and political interests. It is the need for export markets on the part of the industrialised lands, the formal freedom of a world-market and domestic markets which work in favour of the stronger, the expansionism of the multi-national companies, the lop-sided pattern of production and power of the ruling classes in the poor countries themselves, *inter alia*, that distort the ethical stance. It becomes all the clearer how much economic ethics depend on political ethics and how important it is that the process of political liberation should be promoted rather than disturbed by evangelical motives. Selective and temporary dissociation seems at present to be the only means of making the requisite economic control effective. If economic aims are not to reign supreme, these means must be supplemented: the objective must be to promote self-reliance developing in the direction of the establishment of small economic networks and the unfolding of political conditions for a social justice that grows 'from below'.

This is the direction in which most of the articles are moving and to which they contribute partial reflections. This path will be open to the extent that the bearers of economic and political power grow in the awareness that a limitless economic development not only cannot feed the poor from its crumbs, but in the end destroys the rich themselves. This motive of rational self-interest should not, however, be necessary for Christians, for their motives are defined in terms of the radical 'being-for-others' constituted by the existence of Jesus Christ and his conception of God. Further, the maintenance of these motives in practice is what makes the life of the Christian churches in this world credible. To fall short of this constitutes a debt of guilt which can be relieved only by the grace-inspired release into a new practical chance.

DIETMAR MIETH
JACQUES POHIER

Translated by John Maxwell

PART I

Economic Factors in the North-South Conflict

Paul Steidl-Meier

Populations, Environments, Energy and Food Policy: A Problem of Unjust Distribution?

THE TITLE of this article may appear unwieldy; but that is because the subject matter is. The issue is a quadriproblematic (populations-environments-energy-food) and the point is that these four variables are primarily interpreted in terms of each other. Treating them in isolation is folly and yet treating them together is in some ways extraordinarily difficult. Further, the title ends with a question: do they present a problem of unjust distribution? At issue is a problem of systems analysis and the methodology is perforce interdisciplinary. In this introduction I indicate some generally accepted positions regarding this complex system and set out the tasks of the article.

What is being said of the interrelations between populations, environments, energy and food? There is a surprising amount of agreement among observers: there exists a great disequilibrium among various peoples in the world and between present and future anticipated needs.[1] Do these inequalities amount to a problem of unjust distribution? This question frames the task of this article. In fact the precise scope of this article is to show (as best as can be done in a few pages) that the observed disequilibrium is unjust; that it is precisely a *social* injustice; and that more just social policy alternatives are indeed possible. Accordingly, this article discusses the following points:

1. methodology;
2. the scarcity hypothesis;
3. the hypothesis of unjust distribution;
4. alternatives; and
5. conclusion: the Church as participant.

1. METHODOLOGY

Patterns of distribution are tied to social policy and social justice components. In this context, I discuss facts, values and policy.

'The facts' are supposed to describe 'what is'. Yet things are not quite so simple, for

3

what is often called a fact reveals, upon dissection, both constellations of empirically observed phenomena as well as an interpretative framework of those phenomena. The first problem which emerges is that of selectivity in listing the 'relevant' components of an observed phenomena; that is, not all observers give the same description of the facts. Secondly, even if they do, 'data' only exist within a context of ideas and interpretative meaning; that is, 'facts' are interpreted within and compatible with different values and ideologies. In some ways, one's ideology and predisposition help to 'organise' the facts. Policy analysis then becomes framed by the hermeneutic of various beliefs.

These observations are very important in the present context of populations, environments, energy and food. If one examines the traditional Malthusian and Marxist positions, one sees that the Malthusian position interprets the facts as scarcity, brought about on the one hand by excessive population growth and on the other by both environmental and technological limits to growth. The Marxist sees no such scarcity, but rather the concentration of productive sources in the hands of a few resulting in the unmet needs of many. What 'the facts' actually are is of fundamental importance, for in the first case one would develop a morality of scarcity (as seen in 'lifeboat ethics' and notions of 'triage') and in the second one would develop a morality of distribution. The content of what would be considered morally just would accordingly differ in each case. Moral analysis is dependent upon assessment of 'facts'.[2]

But aside from empirical analysis, moral reflection stands upon values. Not just the use-value and exchange-value of goods and services which is familiar to economics, but intrinsic value. Such a notion of fundamental value clearly depends upon articulating an ontology and theological/philosophical anthropology, a view of what one thinks life in general, and human life in particular, is about. Such a task is, however, beyond the scope of this article; suffice it to say that policy cannot be meaningfully analysed without making underlying fundamental values explicit.

An analysis of public policy rests upon an analysis of facts and of moral values. In assessing the facts, one attempts to delineate what has happened and is happening, to grasp the structures and interrelations between events. Such an endeavour rests upon both empirical research and the guiding social science theory and paradigms of that research. The aim of social science in this context of food, populations, energy and environments is to reveal a pattern of distribution and also to demonstrate that other alternative patterns are both possible and better.

Policy is the process of moulding alternative patterns, of shaping what is in the process of becoming. The first step is to specify the ultimate norms (values) which guide policy and set more immediate objectives. The second step is experimentation: designing and testing alternative means to meet one's normative goals and practical objectives, at the same time determining secondary or spill-over effects of policy (which may or may not be desirable). Thus policy, basing itself upon an assessment of the facts and an explicit recognition of guiding values must design means of achieving different patterns of distribution, project all of their potential effects and demonstrate why a particular pattern would be better than alternatives. With this in mind I now examine what are 'the facts' regarding populations, environments, energy and food policy.

2. THE SCARCITY HYPOTHESIS

This section will cover two points:

(a) how many people are hungry and who are they;
(b) why are they hungry.

Estimates about how many people are hungry vary, depending upon operative definitions of malnutrition. According to the Food and Agriculture Organisation some

500-600 million people (roughly 12-15 per cent of world population) suffer from deficiency malnutrition; some 70-90 million (2-3 per cent) are in critical condition. To feed these people well, 30 to 60 million tons of grain (I speak only of grain for the sake of simplicity) would suffice. Yet on reserve in the world's granaries there are nearly 200 million tons; there is no *global* shortage of food.

Yet there are some who, while admitting there is no present food-population problem in a global sense, argue for a relative food-population problem. What is it relative to?

(*a*) Local agriculture productivity; and
(*b*) future expected population.

The FAO (the United Nations Food and Agriculture Organisation) has classified some 44 countries as 'most seriously affected' (MSA); this primarily means that local population growth is outstripping local food production. This fact is affirmed as true; yet one must question this fact in light of other facts, including agricultural production priorities, environment and energy. Economics talks of supply and demand, and we must ask ourselves to what extent the MSA problem is one of excess demand or one of inefficient supply (production and distribution). There are many facts which are seemingly contradictory. First is population density per hectare of agricultural land. According to FAO, Africa and Latin America (where most MSAs are found) in general, use less than 25 per cent of potentially available farmland. In Asia densities are higher, but not that much more so than in Japan or Europe. What is called 'scarcity' is more linked to low yields and poor production technology than to too high a population density. It is primarily a production and marketing problem.

Why are there low yields? To answer this question one must examine the set of inputs used in production. To summarise the matter in an abbreviated fashion they are:

(*a*) land conservation and management, irrigation, and the basic *natural resource endowment*;
(*b*) the available *labour* force and its quality;
(*c*) *capital* (to provide means of production such as tools and fertilisers);
(*d*) *management skills*; and
(*e*) overall *technological resources*.

Numerous studies have been written on each of the above topics. The problem for each country is how to combine its available resources so as to improve food crop yields and overall production. Most poor countries have an adequate natural resource endowment and labour force to achieve these goals, although overall quality needs to be enhanced (through, for example, conservation programmes and rural training and education). The most severe shortages are capital (the debt of poor countries is nearly $300 billion), management skills and access to appropriate technology. The lack of these factors blocks the building up of a science-based agriculture. Yet according to most observers these obstacles to the transformation of traditional agriculture are resolvable, should the political will to do so exist. Even 'poor' India, has grain reserves of some 18 million tons (and has actually sold over 1·5 million tons); furthermore, the Ganges Plain alone has tremendous future potential.

However, even should the technological-production transformation of traditional agriculture take place, the benefits would not automatically reach the poor without a reordering of both social priorities and structures. According to the FAO, there are 4 social groups that suffer most from hunger. They are:

(*a*) the rural landless;
(*b*) the urban unemployed;

B

(c) children; and
(d) pregnant and lactating women.

The hungry are those who neither have the productive resources to produce the food they need, nor the income to enter the market and purchase it; at issue is the distribution of both productive resources as well as food. Furthermore the social position of women and children is one of radical dependence and only compounds their experience of hunger. In this context, a number of policy options is discussed, from transformation of institutions of land tenure and rural credit, to devoting more resources to food production, to non-energy intensive technology so as to provide jobs, to school feeding programmes (unfortunately many poor children do not go to school), to the general social emancipation of women through education and training to population control and so forth. A population policy is necessary, but as a primary solution to the hunger problem, population control is enticingly simple. For the poor and hungry are poor and hungry precisely because they are emarginated; for that reason society's productive resources and surpluses do not flow to them, no matter what their number. Present-day 'scarcity' is both an artificial and systematic product of present socio-economic structures.

The future population problem is more serious. The argument is familiar: it took the world many millions of years to reach a population of 1 billion; but in the last roughly 200 years it has quadrupled to over 4 billion. It is expected to reach 6 billion by the year 2000! Where will it stop and will it stop short of eco-catastrophe and a world war over scarce energy? Population policy is necessary and generally takes two forms: population responsive (migration, planning of services, job creation, etc.) and population influencing (incentives and other means to bring down the birth rate). People have children not simply because of sexual motivation or interpersonal considerations. A wide variety of social motivations figures as well; (such as the future social security of parents, desire for a male offspring, the social position of women, ethnic considerations, child mortality, and distribution of wealth and economic opportunity, to name a few). A significant amount of research has been carried out on these issues; majority opinion seems now to favour population policy within the context of an overall system of public health and an overall improvement in the social-economic quality of people's lives. Whether population control programmes should be left to the free conscience of parents, whether economic incentives and disincentives and restrictive migration policies are moral and so forth are all important questions and continue to be widely debated in population ethics; (however, it is beyond the scope of this paper to review the relevant literature). The point remains, how pressing is the population problem?

It is predicted by UN and FAO sources that population most likely will level off over the next hundred years somewhere near a world population of about 8 to 10 billion people. Such a population could 'adequately' be taken care of with *present* resources and technology. On that most would agree. But the real issue is not 'adequacy' but at what level of affluence and quality of life. At the *present* level of technology, life in the future would be simpler for the countries with large populations than the present quality of affluence in, for example, Western Europe. While in my opinion the scarcity hypothesis does not stand in an absolute sense, the real point is the relative sense of scarcity; i.e., scarcity relative to a *desired* level of affluence. What will be possible in the future depends not only upon schemes of distribution but also upon the development of technology, particularly in finding alternative (and renewable) sources of energy. Opting for ever higher standards of affluence throws one up against many value and general policy dilemmas. To name but a few: a high meat diet leads rich countries to use nearly 80 per cent of their cereals as feed (and therefore they effectively consume 3 to 5 times more than their poor country counterparts); furthermore, consumerism, migration policies, wastage of food, the high energy content of modern 'science-based' systems, food engineering, giving priority to cash exports crops (tea, coffee, etc.) rather than local food production, the control of technology, the distribution of resources, and many related problems make it necessary to examine the 'adequacy versus affluence debate' in light of basic fundamental values which in terms of policy are normative.

In concluding this section I would say that the 'scarcity hypothesis' is by no means easy to evaluate. In reviewing the literature my conclusion is that *present* scarcity is 'artificial' in the sense that it is the product of the system, whether of social structures or inefficient agriculture. The *future* scarcity problem is more complex and one's 'optimism or pessimism' regarding the future depends very much upon one's values and desired quality of life as well as expectations regarding the future shape of technology (especially energy upon which science-based agriculture and 'modern' society is to a large degree based). My conclusion is that, in the context of a projected population of 8 to 10 billion, adequacy (in the sense of meeting basic needs substantially well) is clearly possible and depends mainly upon the political will to solve the problem. The attainment of consumer-society affluence for all is more problematic (should it be even desirable).

3. UNJUST DISTRIBUTION

What is to be produced? How? And for whom? These are the basic questions of food policy in the context of limited environmental resources and supply of energy as well as the demands of population, which stem from both increasing numbers and rising affluence. This section aims to probe whether the unequal distribution we have observed is unjust and, further, whether it is a social injustice.

I have said before that a position on justice is perforce based upon ontological and anthropological considerations. In this article I do not develop these, but in order to speak of injustice I must at least state my criteria. These criteria are based upon the broad tradition of church social teaching. In this teaching (despite elements of pluralism) there are 3 recurrent themes:

(a) the dignity of the human person, based upon being created in God's image;
(b) the universality of creation as seen in the teaching that the world is given to all (and therefore may not be appropriated individualistically); and
(c) individual liberty and self-determination must be related to the common good.

The content of these principles has been debated. But to my mind they do in general lead to a profoundly communitarian ethic, which is distinct both from traditions of liberal democracy and Marxian socialism. It is an ethic of building-up-community, of communion.

There are two orienting principles which guide living in communion: a principle of non-maleficence (to do no harm, as exemplified in the ten commandments) and a principle of beneficence (to do good, even when one has caused no harm, as exemplified in the Samaritan, in the beatitudes and in the very passion and death of the Lord). Such a principle as beneficence is difficult in practice, for it admits of no limits; it is not surprising to see that the spirituality of the Church has often split off from a casuistic morality on this basis. In a summary way, these general orienting principles are the presuppositions which frame my discussion of 4 practical principles of justice: liberty, equality, efficiency and service, and dissent. My position is that the world food system is not working well and that, in fact, it functions maleficently towards the poor; this maleficence derives from human responsibility, as may be seen in examining the practical principle.

First, not all enjoy the freedom of access to the food system, either in terms of having productive resources or of access to market for goods and services. This suppression of freedom contradicts the dignity of the person in negating the possibility of self-determination. In a communitarian framework the liberty of the well-off must be tempered by the common good giving preference to the freedom of the oppressed and granting the same liberty to all.

Second, it is clear that distribution of goods and services in the day to day workings of the food system are grossly unequal. What is more, equality of opportunity, especially for the 4 social groups worst off, is systematically denied. This reality not only contradicts the dignity of the person but the universality of created goods. Furthermore, it overturns both principles of community (non-maleficence and beneficence).

Third, social institutions are to produce a maximum of benefits for the people; the motive for so doing is found in rendering maximum service. The social imperative is to restructure institutions so as to produce more benefits, and that takes more than mere good will and the intention to do so. If one proposes land reform, for example, it is important to realise that small landholders can be more efficient than large ones; but not automatically so. Simultaneous changes are called for in rural credit, extension and markets. And so on with cooperatives and other structural changes; a reductionistic single-factor approach must be eschewed. But the common good does call for institutions which render maximum benefits and service. Present institutions do not do that.

Finally, if a society or system is not just in the sense of liberty, equality and efficient service as specified above, there is then a moral imperative for a prophetic voice, for dissent, for such a system would have lost its legitimacy based upon a communitarian ethic as specified in the principles of non-maleficence and beneficence.

The social injustice of the world food system is seen in lack of access to the system, in unfairly unequal distribution of social economic power and benefits, and in systematic structural inefficiency which fails to produce a maximum of service and furtherance of the common good. Such injustice does not derive from 'fate' or 'fortune' but from human responsibility; not human responsibility in a simple individualistic or even interpersonal sense but in a precisely societal sense. The injustice is embedded in prevailing social patterns and rules of behaviour (whether the 'laws' of the market or the 'rules' of property or of 'realpolitik') and the prevailing values and ideologies which underpin them. Further, they are incarnated in social class and stratification (with its corresponding roles and privileges for different individuals and groups) and enshrined in the various symbolic meaning systems, with their rewards (e.g., Nobel Prizes) and sanctions (arrest for threatening 'national security'). The unjust distribution which has been observed in the nexus of populations, environments, energy and food systems will not be displaced merely by appeals to individual conscience, as important as that may be, but by attacking it in all its societal manifestations as seen in the elements listed above.

4. PROBING ALTERNATIVES

There is no shortage of imaginative alternatives which are also 'logical'; but there is a shortage of good alternatives which would work. World Bank publications, the recent Brandt Commission Report and others talk of changing the terms of trade, of transfer of capital and technology to poor countries, of taxing or eliminating arms sales and so forth. Also, in discussing 'low yields' above, some alternatives were mentioned in the development, implementation and assessment of such policy alternatives. What is thus needed is an 'empirically comprehensive, value-critical approach'. There is not the space to develop in this article some of the concrete alternatives; suffice it to indicate the main elements of this approach.

The criteria of being 'empirically comprehensive' means that one must give attention to the possibility of pertinent data left out or ignored as well as relevant questions ignored.

Furthermore, a 'value-critical approach' calls for open debate on policy goals, fundamental values and the social purpose; for an analysis of conflicts of goals and acceptable tradeoffs; for establishing priorities (as well as the timing and sequence of policy innovations); for assessing constraints (whether deriving from knowledge, or economics or politics) and finally for dividing up responsibilities between international and local participants.

It would be doctrinaire to insist upon a single solution to the populations-environments-energy-food policy problematic. A number of 'policy mixes' is viable; but any approach should attempt to be both empirically comprehensive and value critical. I suggest that the following elements are pertinent to any viable alternative (without at the same time developing such an alternative due to lack of space). The first element concentrates on a critique of prevailing social patterns, their values and ideologies. Such a critique would lead to a transformation of structures; in this case this means to grant the poor access to productive resources (such as land, water, credit, seeds, etc.) and to markets in a manner in which they might determine their own destiny.

Secondly, technological transformation of production and distribution systems is called for such that they become science based without foregoing an 'appropriate' technology. Agricultural, industrial and services sectors of the economy should be simultaneously developed in a complementary way so as to provide stable sources of income to people in the process of economic growth and transformation. In determining access to the system price and income policy (and even rations policy) are of fundamental importance.

Thirdly, in the process of structural change and development in a more technical sense, public policy should be targeted upon improving general welfare in terms of education, nutrition and basic needs such as would be met in a public health programme (of which population policy would form a part). Special emphasis should be given to deprived social groups such as women and children.

These guidelines are general but they do suggest viable policy alternatives. The main obstacle is political will.

5. CONCLUSION: THE CHURCH AS PARTICIPANT

The Church is neither a government nor a corporation. Accordingly its political authority and power in the marketplace is limited. Sociologically, it is primarily a persuasion system; and in this sense it should participate responsibly in the formation of policy.

The Church has long exercised a role in international aid. That is often necessary and often well and good. However, the main point in the populations-environments-energy-food policy problematic is not aid, but social change in building up more just policy and structures.

The first role of the Christian community is to provide an orientation for policy in terms of carrying on a critique of contemporary values and ideologies by which policies and institutions may be evaluated (it goes without saying that some technical competence is called for).

Such a ministry of the Church will truly be social in nature, with various persons in the Church addressing different aspects of the issues. Active participation of all the laity and a truly collegial exercise of ministry in the Church would seem to be a prerequisite (even for methodological reasons alone!).

Thirdly, the Church should be willing to give voice to the masses of the poor who have no effective social voice. Rather than seeming to legitimate unjust structures through silence, the Church must 'spend its social wealth and position' by championing the cause of the poor. To do otherwise would be to fail in its mission of promoting human life, its development and fulfilment. There are no automatic solutions nor a ready-made blueprint for social justice; but to be a responsible participant in a spirit of honest dialogue is a necessary first step if any solutions are to be found for interrelated and pressing local and international problems.

The injustices inherent in the present populations-environments-energy-food policy problematics can and should be addressed in a participatory, collegial manner.

Bibliography

The bibliography which follows is intended for a well-informed introduction to the subject matter in English.

1. Abelson, Phillip, ed. *Food: Politics, Economics, Nutrition and Research* (Washington, D.C. 1975).
Ackroyd, R. *Deficiency Diseases* (WHO 1970).
Brown, Lester *By Bread Alone* (New York 1974).
Coombs *The Assault on World Poverty* (1976).
FAO *Fourth World Food Survey* (Rome 1978).
FAO *Population, Food Supply and Agricultural Development* (Rome 1975).
George, Susan *How the Other Half Dies* (Montclaire, N.J. 1977).
Hopkins, Raymond F. and Puchala, Donald J., eds. *The Global Political Economy of Food* (Madison 1978).
Inst. for Food Policy and Development *Food First, Resource Guide* (San Francisco 1979).
Lappe, Frances Moore and Collins, Joseph *Food First* (Boston 1977).
National Academy of Science (USA) *The World Food and Nutrition Study* (Washington, D.C. 1977—Accompanying this volume we have 5 volumes of supporting papers and a sixth volume on increasing agricultural production in the U.S.).
Reutlinger, Schlomo and Selowsky, Marcelo *Malnutrition and Poverty* (Baltimore 1978).
Reutlinger, Schlomo *'Malnutrition: A Poverty or a Food Problem?'* World Development 5 No. 8 (1977) 715-724.
Sinha, Radha *Food and Poverty* (London 1976).
Tudge, Colin *The Famine Business* (London 1977).
Tuve, George L. *Energy, Environment, Populations and Food* (New York 1976).
United States Department of Agriculture *The World Food Situation and its Prospects to 1985* (Washington 1974).
Wortman, S and Cummings, R. *To Feed This World* (Baltimore 1979).

2. Aiken, William and LaFollette, Hugh *World Hunger and Moral Obligation* (Englewood Cliffs 1977).
Freudenberger, C. Dean and Minus, Paul M., Jr. *Christian Responsibility in a Hungry World* (Nashville 1977).
Gremillion, Joseph, ed. *Food, Energy and the Major Faiths* (New York 1978).
Islam, Nural *World Food Strategy: Ethics, Politics and Policy* (London 1976).

Jegan, Mary Evelyn and Manno, Bruno *The Earth is the Lord's: Essays on Stewardship* (New York 1979).

Jegen, Mary Evelyn and Wilbur, Charles *Growth with Equity* (New York 1979).

Lucas, George R., Jr. and Ogletree, Thomas E., eds. *Lifeboat Ethics* (New York 1976).

Simon, Arthur *Bread for the World* (New York 1979).

Winter, Gibson *Elements for a Social Ethic* (New York 1971).

Wogaman, J. Philip *The Great Economic Debate: An Ethical Analysis* (Philadelphia 1977).

Wogaman, J. Philip, ed. *The Population Crisis and Moral Responsibility* (New York 1973).

Siro Lombardini

Inequalities in the
World Trade System
(Price, Protectionism, Growth Processes)

1. A SPECTACLE OF CONTRASTS: DEVELOPMENT AND UNDERDEVELOPMENT

THE COMING of capitalism to Europe and North America gave rise to a new international division of labour causing unprecedentedly severe disequilibria in the international economic system, with some features that appear irreversible. On the one hand there are the underdeveloped countries that are selling raw materials whereby the developed countries can enrich themselves; on the other hand there are the countries that have a monopoly of industry, possessors of capital and controllers of the international monetary system. It is widely held that only by means of economic growth can Third World countries break out of the strait-jacket in which they have been placed by the way in which the world economy has developed. As long as they remain thus confined, political independence will only produce frustration, resentment and the exacerbation of racial frictions—the very conditions that are needed to ensure the persistence of the new colonial order. The colonial régime has become even more necessary to the capitalist system since new discoveries have rendered indispensable certain raw materials, such as uranium, that are only found in sufficient quantities in African and Asian countries, and since the alarming prospect of a serious shortage of petroleum and other sources of energy has loomed on the horizon.

Thus the ideal of political independence in fact rather than in name has come to be closely associated with the ideal of economic growth, because this will enable Third World countries both to integrate their ethnic minorities and also to negotiate with developed countries, if not on an equal footing, at least not on terms of complete and permanent inferiority—in other words, to become full members of the international community.

2. SOME OF THE KNOTS TO BE UNRAVELLED

The moral implications of inequalities that, in the view of the writer, can and should be overcome by economic growth, appear inescapable when stated in the above terms. Everything likely to favour growth in Third World countries leading to the elimination of internal inequalities and those subsisting between Third World and capitalist countries, is ethically desirable. Everything that accentuates the inequality and places obstacles in the path of their realisation is to be deplored. In practice, however, it is not as easy to arrive at a valid moral judgment as might be thought if one accepts the problem of inequalities and growth as set out above. To be precise:

(*a*) Even if the foregoing interpretation is accepted, two problems remain to be overcome. We have to identify those activities that aggravate the inequalities and put a brake on development, and those that have the contrary effect. We also have to pinpoint the individuals and groups (classes and categories) whose decisions influence the possibility of avoiding the adverse effects and promoting the favourable ones. The extreme difficulty of solving this problem becomes apparent when we consider:

   (i) that what has to be assessed, especially in the case of collectivities, is not the logical (or technical) possibility of making choices which reduce inequality and promote development, but the possibility of doing so *in the real world*; and
  (ii) in certain historical situations, antagonisms may arise in the pursuit of a higher growth rate and a lessening of economic inequality.

Inequality can be defined in mechanistic terms, but these are not appropriate. Apart from the difficulty of deciding when we can speak of the equal distribution of income among people whose tastes differ, it is doubtful whether a *just* society can be equated with one in which incomes are equally distributed. In practice, inequality is held to be unjust if, and in so far as, it results from the exploitation of some citizens by others. But exploitation is hard to define and even harder to measure. Even the concepts of growth and development cannot be so unambiguously defined as is often imagined.

(*b*) The problem of inequality and retarded development in Third World countries is inseparable from that of new types of exploitation and the present outlook for advanced capitalist systems (on which I contributed an article in 1978).

I shall continue the present article with some reflections on the points touched upon under (*b*), endeavouring to give examples of some kinds of exploitation which help to explain the inequality and the obstacles to economic growth in Third World countries. As far as space allows, I shall emphasise the part played by prices and protectionism.

3. THE PROBLEM OF EXPLOITATION

One of the key arguments in Marx's theory of value is the affirmation that under a capitalist system the degree of exploitation of the labour force tends to become equalised throughout the various sectors. Modern developments in theory have shown that this statement is true only for an economy that is growing at a constant, uniform rate. This theoretical growth curve may be distorted either by the tendency in a competitive system for the rates of profit in different industries to be evened out, or by the formation of monopoly situations. Hence the rate of profit cannot be taken as a measure of the exploitation of the workers by capitalists. It would be more accurate to say that a relationship cannot be defined between the behaviour of a class (the capitalist class) and the exploitation of other classes (workers). The truth is that exploitation occurs in many directions and takes effect through relationships, sometimes complex, caused by many interactive mechanisms. Workers are exploited, for instance, not only as workers but also as consumers. Direct exploitation of the worker is accompanied by indirect exploitation, which is shaped by the structure of market power. These two types of exploitation are not simply superimposed on one another; sometimes they are not even logically distinguishable.

These considerations assume major importance when the international economic system is involved. The crisis affecting the capitalist systems has brought into play homeostatic mechanisms tending to maintain the distribution of revenue in harmony with the requirements of growth within each national economy and in the international economy. These mechanisms have made it easy to detect the main if not the only active ingredient of exploitation in the capitalist class; but they have made it even more difficult to pinpoint the origin and the forms of exploitation. Indeed, some kinds of exploitation are practised by sections of the working class to the detriment of other sections of the working class, whilst within the capitalist class conflicts of interest are tending to take on fresh emphases and meanings.

4. SOME SPECIFIC FORMS OF EXPLOITATION: THE NEW COLONIALISM

It is not possible to measure the extent to which a given class or group is subjected to exploitation; in practice, one and the same group may be the exploiter in some relationships and the exploited in others. Nevertheless, it is possible to identify some particular forms of exploitation set up by specific mechanisms, among which are the following:

(a) The price formation and wages mechanism

(i) One specific type of exploitation takes place as a result of the formation of monopoly situations in industrialised countries, which are then able to offer some of their products on the world market at prices in excess of costs in exchange for products which Third World countries have to offer in competitive markets, and which are therefore sold at prices equal to costs.

(ii) A second type of exploitation occurs as a result of the lower wage levels ruling in Third World countries. Two cases have to be distinguished here: first, goods are sold in world markets at uniform prices equal to the costs incurred in countries where wages are higher (this case usually occurs when production is carried out in low-wage countries by multinational companies which are thus able to make high profits: see under (b) (ii) and (iii); second, the goods are sold in world markets at prices equal to the costs incurred in the Third World countries in which all or most of the production is carried out, and in this case we can speak of unequal exchange and of exploitation of the poor countries by the rich ones.

These forms of exploitation have been turned upside down in part during the last decade by the use that some raw materials producer countries (of petroleum in particular) have made of the strongly inelastic demand and their resultant market power. This, however, has resulted not only in worsening the crisis of the capitalist countries in some of its aspects, but also in dividing Third World countries into those producing such raw materials and those which do not have them and which in consequence have suffered increased exploitation.

(b) The mechanisms regulating international distribution of investments

Certain investments in Third World countries can be undertaken only by enterprises from highly industrialised countries (take as an example the exploitation of the Chilean copper mines). Thus the distribution of investments, even more than the flows of international trade, reflects the distribution of economic power. This involves specific forms of exploitation:

(*i*) At the time at which the investment is made, in that certain natural resources of the host country are acquired at extremely low prices reflecting the monopoly demand of the investing country.

(*ii*) In benefits from the structure of production, in that advantage is taken of the very low wage levels obtainable in the underdeveloped country.

(*iii*) In the application of profits, which generally are spent largely outside the country in which they are earned. Because of this, the bringing into production of such resources as mines has in general had only a limited effect on the rate of growth in Third World countries. Another reason is that the creation of the necessary transport infrastructure, notably ports, has made it easier to import foreign goods that could be paid for by exports.

(*c*) Finance flows

Third World countries are not in a position to balance their foreign trade; their *payments* are balanced by loans granted in various ways by industrialised countries. This means that Third World countries have to devote part of their resources to producing export commodities in order to pay the interest on the loans they have contracted. Usually these loans have to be rolled over or renewed, a fact which emphasises the relationship of dependence *vis-à-vis* industrialised countries. With the advent of consumer-orientated capitalism, two further forms of exploitation have come into special prominence.

(*d*) The overseas siting of facilities and the activation of local processes of industrialisation, subordinated to the strategies of the multinationals

For a number of reasons (not least the possibility of employing local labour at substantially lower rates of pay than those prevailing in industrialised countries to produce goods increasingly intended for supplying the markets in the latter) the large multinational companies are setting up new enterprises in Third World countries. This is resulting in a new division of labour, with white collar workers increasing in the industrialised countries and blue collar workers in Third World countries. Then industrialisation is represented to the Third World countries as synonymous with economic growth. And as Lewis forecast theoretically in 1954, the traditional, mainly agricultural sector becomes nothing more than a reservoir of labour. Furthermore this labour does not filter into industry at a rate that maintains some sort of balance between the sectors—which is what Lewis expected to happen; instead, people decamp in droves, causing agriculture to stagnate or even regress. With agriculture thus weakened, and further impeded by tariff barriers and agricultural policies adopted by the industrialised countries, sustained economic development which could form the basis for the implementation of growth strategies sufficiently independent of those imposed by the multinationals, becomes impossible.

(*e*) The export of technologies and of cultural patterns evolved in the West

In this way the economic power of the industrialised countries that have developed these technologies and are most favourably placed for producing the goods called for by the new cultural patterns, is reinforced. There are also some changes in the structure of duties and tariffs favouring this strategic design of limiting the growth possibilities for Third World countries, and affecting their ability to sustain and develop their own cultural identity. These include in particular the tendency of countries where multinationals are located to promote the formation of common market areas in those parts of the world—Europe and Latin America—where there exists sufficient potential demand to justify starting up new plants of adequate size.

5. THE OBSTACLES TO ECONOMIC GROWTH

The particular kinds of exploitation referred to above are inimical to self-sustaining growth. Other causes of specific hindrances have been:

(a) support for political structures likely to ensure a subservient pattern of economic development of the above-mentioned types: the capitalist countries have made this possible in Third World countries;

(b) integrating the local bourgeoisie with the bourgeoisie in capitalist countries—a process encouraged by the export of cultural patterns from the latter to Third World countries; and

(c) the indoctrination of technicians and engineers, including those coming from Third World countries to study at British and American universities, whose skills are needed to promote any sort of economic growth. It is sufficient to recall that economic growth generally resolves itself into a macro-economic contest without taking into account structural changes, some of which are *valuable* either because they represent a *result* in and for themselves of the development process or because, since they are conducive to growth, they are judged in the same way as investments. If investment is looked upon as synonymous with growth, the equilibrium theory continues to be accepted so readily that it leads to neglect of the disequilibria caused by development models *exported* from the capitalist countries. And it is precisely in relation to these disequilibria that there is need to rethink the strategy of economic and social development. What is needed is development capable of improving the prospects of growth while preserving stability and without putting the social and cultural objectives at risk if introduced in parallel in the manufacturing sector (through modern industrialisation) and in the traditional sector (in which other manufacturing activities could be conjoined with agricultural pursuits). In essence, this is the development pattern that has been adopted in China. In the end, the obstacles to growth provoke reactions that open up new prospects for Third World countries. But unless the problems arising from the links between the crises of the capitalist countries and possible lines of development for Third World countries are resolved, these prospects will not be able to be actualised in a satisfactory and stable manner.

6. INTERNATIONAL ECONOMIC RELATIONS, CRISIS OF CAPITALIST SYSTEMS AND THE PROSPECTS FOR DEVELOPING COUNTRIES

We have examined the fluctuations in the terms of trade to find evidence of exploitation and obstacles to self-sustaining growth in Third World countries. But it must be said at once that it is not easy to interpret the raw data, not only because of the difficulty of constructing price indices but also because of the difficulty, at first sight, of identifying curves that can be considered as *normal* (and impartial) to use as yardsticks for assessment of the empirically observed fluctuations. The importance of the terms of trade becomes obvious when it is realised that exports by non-communist under-developed countries represent amounts varying from 15 to 30 per cent of their Gross National Product.

As Bairoch pointed out in 1975, contrary to a widely held belief there has been an improvement in the relative prices of raw materials during the past hundred years. This, however, does not invalidate our comments on the mechanisms tending to accentuate the exploitation of Third World countries, or at any rate, of a large number of them. For it is reasonable to suppose that in the absence of these mechanisms of exploitation the relative prices of raw materials would have shown a more consistent increase, in so far as their production has not enjoyed the full benefits of the cost-saving technological improvements applied to manufactured exports from the industrialised countries.

Various proposals have been put forward in an endeavour to stabilise and support the prices of raw materials. Unfortunately they have so far remained in the realm of wishful thinking. There are indeed some signs of impending change, but these are due not to international agreements but to changes in the international division of labour that have thrown some industries, such as steelmaking, into crisis, and to the way in which some raw materials producing countries (notably of petroleum) have exploited their market power. It is, however, difficult to foresee a situation of *normalisation* of international economic relationships resulting from the processes at present under way.

Only if the capitalist countries, having overcome their own crises, are led to adopt a pattern of development which includes a greater emphasis on old and new social services will there be an opportunity of taking a fresh look at the tariff systems and of instituting processes of adjustment in the agricultural and industrial sectors of the various countries, so as to create the elbow-room in the world economy that is needed to implement strategies of development suitable for adoption by Third World countries. And those countries themselves must realise that such strategies cannot be implemented unless they create the internal political and cultural conditions that are needed for their fruition.

Translated by Alan Braley

Bibliography

Bairoch, Paul *The Economic Development of the Third World since 1900* (London 1975).
Brookfield, H. *Interdependent Development* (London 1975).
Emmanuel, A. *L'Echange inégal. Essai sur les antagonismes dans les rapports économiques internationaux* (Paris 1969).
Furtado, Celso *Gli stati uniti e il sottosviluppo dell'America Latina* (Milano 1975).
Lewis, W. A. 'Economic Development with Unlimited Supply of Labour' in *The Economics of Underdevelopment* ed. A. N. Agarwala and S. P. Song (Oxford 1958).
Lombardini, S. 'Crisi del sistema (capitalistico) e crisi dell' economia' in *Nur Oekonomie ist keine Oekonomie* ed. P. Caroni, B. Dafflon, G. Enderle (Berne and Stuttgart 1978).
Myrdal, G. *Asian Drama: An Inquiry into the Poverty of Nations* (London 1968).

Hanns Abele

Financial Aspects of North-South Relations

1. INTRODUCTION: THE PREVAILING WORLD ECONOMIC ORDER

INTERNATIONAL economic relations are determined by both real and monetary factors. Real factors include, besides the size of countries, the extent to which they are equipped with the means of production, their possession of raw materials, their population, the level of technical know-how (which in turn establishes the techniques of production that are used), and the level of demand. Monetary or financial elements include the internal money supply, the level of taxation, the structure of the banking system and its state of development, and the exchange rate, that is the relationship between internal and external currencies. The balance of transactions between home and abroad is termed the balance of payments and provides information about a country's international position. If exports exceed imports, the proceeds can be regarded as an international reserve. From another point of view the balance of payments also provides an indication of movements of capital. If a country receives a loan on the international financial markets this means an increase in its international means of payment but as far as its wealth is concerned creates an obligation requiring the payment of interest and the repayment of the capital.

The institutional framework within which international economic relations are conducted is established by the regulations governing trade and the international monetary order. For its evolution and supervision institutions or organs have been set up to guarantee the legal security and confidence without which international transactions would not be able to take place at all. From the historical point of view the present world economic order is the expression of the balance of political and economic power and changes according to shifts in the market positions of individual countries or groups of countries. In this way the present form of the world economic order—with institutions like the International Monetary Fund (IMF), the World Bank, GATT (General Agreement on Tariffs and Trade), or UNCTAD (United Nations Conference on Trade and Development), OPEC (Organisation of Petroleum Exporting Countries), OECD (Organisation for Economic Co-operation and Development)—is the result of the relationships existing at the end of World War II and of developments since then.

It is important to remember that because of the mutual interdependence of national economies, something that in the process of economic development is on the increase as the result of differentiation and the division of labour, certain transfer mechanisms have been institutionalised by the world economic order. As long as a system of fixed exchange rates predominated, people spoke of 'imported' inflation, by which they understood the transfer of rises in the level of prices from one country to another. Since the transition to a system of flexible exchange rates people are aware that the disadvantage of the transfer of inflation was balanced by an advantage in the form of the stimulation of a boom, an advantage that has now disappeared. If, for example, the American economy was heading towards a boom then, thanks to the system of fixed exchange rates, these stimulating effects were transferred to Europe and the developing countries without their having to make efforts in this direction. Hence it is very difficult to establish whether developments are caused by real rather than monetary factors of *vice versa*. On the other hand it is certainly not possible to neglect the purely financial aspects in any analysis of the international economy.

2. THE FINANCIAL ASPECTS OF NORTH-SOUTH RELATIONSHIPS

From 1973 onwards the fourfold increase in the price of oil has stimulated increased interest in one particular question concerning the financial relations between industrialised and developing nations: the steady increase in the latter's indebtedness. Since there are various differing opinions on this problem, the basic issue will first of all be presented quite abstractly in a simplified form.

(a) The regulation of financing

In an economy in which goods or services can be obtained only against money, demand presupposes suitable means of payment, which in turn limits the extent to which goods can be obtained, whether for consumption or investment. If now credits are placed at the disposal of an economic unit such as a country, then it is able to obtain more than would have been permitted by the means of payment available to it at the moment. Credit thus expands the opportunities of action open to debtors. But because in contrast to gifts loans have to be repaid, and because over and above this interest has to be paid for the use of this finance for a period of time, the judgment whether loans are sensible or not depends on the use to which the money is put. If, for example, someone receives 100 units of account and uses these simply to increase his consumption, then he may enjoy a momentary increase in satisfaction, but he has no means for paying the interest and repaying the loan in the future. These payments can only be achieved by means of a painful reduction in his accustomed level of consumption and thus by additional cuts and retrenchment. The hope of being able to outwit one's creditors is, at least in the world of international finance, very small, since no one can be found to place further loans at the disposal of a debtor who is dilatory in making his payments: every new creditor must reckon with the possibility that his loan too will not be repaid. The situation is quite different when the loan is used for investment. If the 100 units of account are used to obtain a machine, the repayment of the loan and the payment of interest on it can be made out of the proceeds earned by the machine—provided that a market can be found for the goods the machine produces and provided they can be sold at suitable prices.

(b) The indebtedness of the developing countries and its influence on development

If these considerations are now applied to international loans to developing countries, it will be recognised that the phenomenon of indebtedness is not on its own sufficient to categorise the position of the developing countries. First of all the use to which loans are applied enables one to evaluate whether indebtedness could be advantageous for the developing countries. Since the larger part of the total indebtedness of developing countries is concentrated in a few countries, at least as far as debts to private creditors are concerned, and since these are among the most highly developed of the developing countries with higher Gross National Product per head (Brazil and Mexico are examples), it is repeatedly argued that there can be no talk of the developing countries having too great a burden of debt. On this argument it is precisely because of their comparatively higher state of development that these countries are to a greater extent dependent on the import of foreign capital in order to be able to execute their ambitious programmes of development. The other side of the coin is that this enables them to become industrialised, to earn the revenue they need from the proceeds of exports, and thereby to pay off the debt as well as paying the interest on it.

This line of argument stresses two aspects. Whether the developing countries are indeed suffering from too great a burden of indebtedness is not a question that can be answered by lumping them all together. It is only by investigating them country by country that one will be able to find out the extent to which we can expect developments dangerous for an individual country or for the world economy as a whole. Further, the credit needs of a country depend on its state of development: accelerated development means greater demand for credit but also an improved ability to repay the loan, or, in banking jargon, less risk of default or higher creditworthiness.

(i) *The poorest developing countries*

Although the situation of individual countries can be very different, there are developments that affect groups of countries. After the quadrupling of the price of oil in 1973, developing countries with the lowest *per capita* income and without their own supplies of oil encountered great difficulties with regard to their balance of payments: they were suddenly faced with the need to pay out more for their imports of oil without being able to bring about a corresponding increase in their exports and thus earn the necessary means to be able to go on importing oil. If they had received no loans they would suddenly have been deprived of oil as a source of energy. This would have led to an abrupt adjustment that could have given rise to structural collapse in the process of development and could have had partially catastrophic effects on the population. Settlement of their balance of payments difficulties did admittedly make possible an extension of the time available to make the adjustments that were needed but did not remove the necessity of making changes. These changes needed to aim at restoring the balance of payments at least in the mid-term, and, following what has been said above, this called for either an increase in exports or a reduction in imports or both. If, however, the developing countries taken as a group are not able to increase their exports because owing to a recession demand for goods exported by developing countries has stagnated or even fallen back in the industrialised countries, then the only solution remains that of reducing imports. But if imported goods are essential for development or even simply to maintain the present level of existence, then it is easy to see what the consequences of this kind of enforced adjustment will be.

(ii) *The most advanced developing countries*

The second argument, too—that only those countries that can afford it are deeply in debt—involves an oversimplification of the entire situation. Lumping all the developing countries together has just as little validity when it comes to looking at their various situations of indebtedness. One quite important factor that differentiates them is the conditions attached to the loans granted to individual countries as well as the periods for which individual loans are made and the dates on which they fall due. Besides loans granted within the framework of official development aid—loans which carry a low rate of interest, which do not have to be repaid for a longer term of years, and which are often transformed into outright gifts—the financing of developing countries has in the 1970s been increasingly effected by means of the international financial market or by the major banks. The conditions for these loans follow the situation on the international financial markets. Under normal conditions it is possible for those countries that have received market loans of this kind to replace loans that have expired by new ones. But if their loans have repayment terms that allow an increased demand for finance to arise within a relatively short time, or if for a variety of reasons the international money markets are not very forthcoming, or if the granting of loans by banks to a particular country or group of countries has already reached a high total, crises of liquidity can arise. Although the mid-term creditworthiness of the more developed developing countries cannot be disputed, they are not immune to such problems. Since finance arranged through the money markets is short-term and is expensive for the debtor, the possibility of this kind of crisis cannot be excluded.

The danger does not arise for the poorer developing countries, since they have no access to private sources of finance: they represent too great a risk for the creditor. Their balance of payments problems can only be tided over by an increase in the level of development aid. But the level of public, official development aid given by the industrialised countries has failed to reach the targets that have been set. This is the outcome both of the lack of public support for the transfer of capital within the framework of development aid and of the slackening of the economic tempo in the industrialised countries, leading to a decline in readiness to rearrange expenditure or take on new expenditure for the benefit of those who are economically weak.

(c) The role of the fluctuation of prices on the international markets

The proceeds the developing countries earn from their exports, as well as their expenditure on imports, and thus their balance of payments, are very persistently affected by the fluctuation of prices on the international markets. If there is a fall in the prices paid for raw materials or products mainly exported by the developing countries, then there is a decline in the value of a country's exports even when the volume of exports remains the same. The effects of this fall in prices are intensified if it is accompanied by an increase in the prices charged for imports. Inflation in the industrialised countries has its effects on the developing countries through the increase in the prices of industrial products. They are able to import quantitatively fewer industrial products for the same amount that they earn from their exports. The organisation of the international currency system is an important factor for the transfer of inflationary imports, since it also influences the possibility of guarding against the negative influence of fluctuations in prices, sales and finance by building up reserves. The argument that the industrialised countries too must share an interest in establishing stable prices for raw materials so as to safeguard their long-term interests has been used by the developing countries in the dialogue between North and South in an attempt to obtain guaranteed prices or incomes. A comprehensive agreement on raw materials would serve this purpose. But in the long term it seems dubious whether the major political investment that would be needed to bring such an agreement about would in fact best serve the long-term interest of the developing countries. The more progress they make on the road of industrialisation, the more dependent they become on the sale of their new products in the industrialised countries and are thus concerned more with the prices they obtain for finished products than for the raw materials that represent the chief source of income for undeveloped countries. Opinions differ about the future development of the state of trade and the relative prices of industrial products and of agricultural produce or raw materials. But this analysis shows that it is not only absolute

c

price levels and changes in them (inflation, changes in exchange rates) but also changes in the relative prices of various groups of goods that are significant for the relative position of different groups of countries.

3. THE RELATIVE INTERESTS OF CREDITOR AND DEBTOR COUNTRIES

From the financial point of view it is also necessary to analyse the various interests held by different countries in order to reach a judgment on the effects of economic inequality. In this the industrialised countries occupy the position of creditors. They provide development aid—in the 1970s the OPEC countries provided increased development aid—and finance balance of payments problems. The International Monetary Fund provides in this context a court of appeal which supervises the progress of the process of adjustment. From the point of view of the developing countries the short time-scales demanded by the IMF and the hardships these bring about very often seem excessive, because they see the IMF as the representative of the creditor nations and only in extreme instances lay claim to the opportunities for credit it provides. For the major banks, which to a large extent have in the 1970s taken on the financing of balances of payments, this extension of their business represents a welcome addition, since they were exposed to a heavy influx of funds from OPEC countries and were looking for suitable investment. So far this expansion of their business has been very profitable and the risk limited. Since the major international banks also dominate the financial structures of the industrialised countries, any crisis in the field of the financing of the developing countries would certainly not remain without its effects on the industrialised countries.

On the other hand the industrialised countries cannot sell their products in the developing countries if the latter cannot finance these imports. This consideration has given rise to the various forms of export credits which are designed to serve this purpose. As creditors the industrialised nations are thus interested in the repayment of their loans and thus implicitly in the uses to which these are put. The risk of a fall in prices, a change in the exchange rate or a drop in demand affects the debtor country first of all. But on the other hand a particularly efficient use of capital leads to the developing countries penetrating the markets of the industrialised countries with their products and thus causing problems of redundancy in some branches of industry and some regions. The response of the industrialised countries to these difficulties is to try to meet them by increased protectionist measures, all of which aim at stemming the inflow of goods. But what is evident from what has been said above is that this will endanger the repayment of loans that have already been made and thus increase the problem of the indebtedness of the developing countries *vis-à-vis* the industrialised nations.

The debtor countries are as a group marked by opposing interests. These differ according to the extent to which they are endowed with natural resources (oil-producing countries contrasted with the rest) and according to their stage of development. As far as the poorest countries are concerned, an increase in the provision of development aid is the most important. In this it should be observed that the general acceleration of inflation has sharply reduced the purchasing power of the sums involved in development aid, so that nominal increases can mean a reduction in real terms. Those countries that rely more on private loans arranged through the money markets are more interested in access to these markets and in loans with long periods of repayment and low levels of interest. Although the demand for a general reduction of debt is often raised, the developing countries themselves are far from agreed on this. Fulfilment of this demand in fact hides the risk that those countries providing loans will be much less forthcoming in future, which would affect those countries that rely on this form of finance.

The significance attaching to financial relationships between industrialised countries and developing countries depends on the economic order, the pattern of development and the system of values implicit in them. More technical discussions should not divert attention from the fact that basically what is to be solved is a problem of distribution, a question that arises in the same way on the international as on the national level. In this context it should finally be recalled that it is not by accident that it was a group of Scottish moral theologians who are among the founders of modern economics.

Translated by Robert Nowell

Bibliography

(1) Introductory reading:

Aronson, J. D., ed. *Debt and the Less Developed Countries* (Boulder 1979)

Wellons, P. A. *Borrowing by Developing Countries on the Euro-Currency Markets* (OECD, Paris 1977).

(2) Source material and studies:

OECD *External Indebtedness of Developing Countries: Present Situation and Future Prospects* (Paris 1979).

The International Bank for Reconstruction and Development/The World Bank *World Development Report* (Washington, D.C. August 1979).

(3) General bibliography:

United Nations Library, Geneva, Publications Series C *Debt Problems of Developing Countries* (Geneva 1979).

Roger Riddell

Transnational Corporations and Technology and Their Effects on Poverty, Income Distribution and Employment in Less Developed Countries

1. THE INEQUALITIES BETWEEN 'NORTH' AND 'SOUTH'

THE WORLD today is characterised by widespread poverty in the less developed countries (LDCs) and a huge gap in wealth and income between rich and poor countries and within poor countries.

(a) Poverty—Wealth

Four-fifths of the world's income is earned by the industrialised nations of the world, North America, western and eastern Europe, where only one-quarter of the world's population lives. Amidst mass provision of basic services of education, health and social security, average life expectancy in these countries, often referred to as the 'North', is about 70 years. In contrast, average life expectancy among the poor nations of the world—the 'South'—is less than 50 years. In the South's poorest nations, 1 child in 4 dies before reaching the age of 5 and over 50 per cent are destined for lifelong illiteracy. In the South today, 800 million people live in conditions of absolute poverty or destitution, with some 500 million suffering from a severe degree of protein malnutrition. But not all those living in the South are poor and inequalities within these countries are large: in most LDCs, the richest 10 per cent of households receive 40 per cent of national income and the poorest 40 per cent receive less than 15 per cent.

In general, the countries of the South are suppliers of raw materials to the North and they play a minor role in worldwide manufacturing. The North is responsible for over 90 per cent of world exports, 85 per cent of arms production, 98 per cent of all research and development while consuming 87 per cent of world energy and 80 per cent of world fertilisers. International trade agreements are dominated by the interests of countries of the North which have the power to control most international trade fora.

(b) The growing inequality

A second feature of the prevailing world order is growing inequality: the gap between the rich and poor nations is increasing while the distribution of wealth and income within poor countries is, in general, tending to become even more skewed in favour of the more affluent. This phenomenon is clear from recent statistical trends. For example, between 1960 and 1970, 80 per cent of the world's increased production of wealth accrued to countries where income per head in 1960 was over US$1,000. The share in world trade of the non-oil-exporting LDCs fell from 19 per cent in 1960 to 14 per cent in 1975. In a world of international inflation which results in the increasing relative cost of manufactured goods which the LDCs need to import, poor countries are finding it more and more difficult to make ends meet. The balance of payments deficits of non-oil-exporting LDCs will have risen from US$11 billion in 1963 to an estimated US$200 billion by the end of 1980 while their external debt quadrupled from US$74 billion in 1970 to US$320 billion in 1978.

Not only is there a huge problem of lack of employment opportunities in poor countries—some 35 per cent of the working population of LDCs is considered to be either unemployed or seriously underemployed—but about half of the increase in the labour force in the last 20 years can be classified as destitute or seriously poor. Most countries of the South have high rates of population growth, often as high as 3 per cent a year, so equivalent rates of economic growth are necessary just to maintain average levels of income. But even when growth rates are high, it is often the case that poorer groups have become worse off, relatively and sometimes absolutely. Recent evidence (though some of this is admittedly scanty) suggests that over time the incomes of the lowest 40 per cent of people in LDCs and especially the poorest 2 per cent have decreased even when average incomes have been rising. One example of the economic growth 'miracle' is Brazil where after 10 years of rapid growth, the share of national income of the top 5 per cent rose from 29 to 36 per cent and that of the poorest 40 per cent fell from 10 to 8 per cent.

Widespread poverty in the Third World and growing inequality both on the world level and within countries of the South are now widely acknowledged and are leading to statements by influential leaders in northern countries, as well as in the South, condemning present patterns of growth and development and calling for fundamental change. Robert McNamara, President of the World Bank, has commented that:

> "the state of development in most developing countries today is unacceptable and growing more so . . . because development programmes have been directed at gross economic goals and have failed to ensure that all nations have shared equitably in economic advance."[1]

More recently, the 1980 Report of the Brandt Commission has pointed out that 'in the world, as in nations, economic forces left entirely to themselves tend to produce growing inequalities'.[2]

2. THE EFFECTS OF THE TRANSNATIONAL CORPORATIONS ON THIRD WORLD DEVELOPMENT

It is against this background that we shall consider here the effects that transnational corporations (TNCs) have on Third World development. As we shall see, not only have these corporations come to play an increasingly important role in shaping the world economy, but they also make the most significant contribution to the transfer of technology from the rich North to the poor South. In particular, we shall examine the ways that TNCs and the availability, access and distribution of technology affect income and employment levels and overall patterns of development in the Third World.

(a) The Economic and Technological Dominance of the North

Transnational corporations can be loosely defined as enterprises whose activities are carried out in two or more countries. They include enterprises involved in the agricultural, manufacturing, mining, transportation, insurance and banking sectors whose activities involve extraction of raw materials, processing, industrial production, marketing and finance. In the last 30 years, TNCs have come to dominate practically all major economic activities. Between one-quarter and one-third of all world production originates in the TNCs and some 30 per cent of world trade takes place within different branches of these corporations. A small number of large TNCs dominate the marketing and processing of a number of the world's key economic resources such as oil, bauxite, copper, iron ore, nickel, tin, zinc, bananas, sugar and tea. But the economic power of TNCs goes well beyond these more visible manifestations; TNCs dominate the world's banking system, they are involved in widespread subcontracting agreements with local enterprises, the global sourcing of different parts of the production process in low-income countries and in massive international retailing.

Not surprisingly in a world dominated by the industrialised countries of the North, one finds that the North has an almost total global monopoly of economic know-how and technology and in a world where western-based TNCs are so influential, one finds that TNCs play the dominant role in the development and allocation of technology to the poor South. Indeed, perhaps the principal contribution of private TNCs to host countries and their main source of market power lies in their technology.

(b) The Technological Hegemony of the TNCs

The scale of global technology and its distribution is apparent from the following. In 1976, it was estimated that the global value of technology was some US$11 billion; of this, LDCs had a 10 per cent share. At present, the LDCs' bill for technology amounts to about half the direct flow of private investment into their countries each year. In 1972, United States' firms alone received over US$2·7 billion in overseas receipts for royalties and fees associated with technology transfer and of this, over 90 per cent accrued to TNCs. That the present inequalities in the availability of technology are likely to increase is evident when it is realised that as much as 98 per cent of world spending on research and development takes place in the North, largely within TNCs. Most technologies when they are first introduced are covered by patents; in 1972, of 3·5 million patents in existence only 6 per cent were granted to LDCs and in that year of the total number of patents held in LDCs over 90 per cent were never used.

The *raison d'etre* of a TNC in its general operations and in the access it gives to its technology, like any other capitalist enterprise, is to ensure the long-term profit levels of the corporation. Compared with indigenous enterprise in poor countries, TNCs are highly efficient and because of their technical know-how, their experience in world-wide production and marketing and their enormous investment capabilities, they are able to expand rapidly and to adapt quickly to changes in world economic demand, by shifting from one type of activity to another or by moving from one part of the world to another. It is because of these characteristics that TNCs have been able to expand with such rapidity into the underdeveloped South.

Because of these characteristics there are, not surprisingly, many immediate attractions which foreign investment in general and TNCs in particular offer to LDCs. Like aid flows, the foreign capital that TNCs bring to a country provides an immediately favourable effect to its international balance of payments position. TNCs also bring with them efficient technical processes, machinery and consumer goods from the affluent North—the visible signs of modernity which would otherwise be largely unobtainable to the poor nations of the world. Finally, TNCs provide employment in LDCs for both skilled and unskilled workers; it has been estimated that currently TNCs provide directly some 2 million jobs in the Third World.

(c) The Harmful Effects of the Hegemony of the TNCs

Attractive though these immediate benefits are, there has been an increasing awareness in recent years of the harmful effects that TNCs, their activities and their production processes bring to the South. In a world characterised by large and growing inequalities, the uncontrolled activities of northern-based TNCs tend to stifle indigenous activity, to check the potential development of locally-based technologies and products, to exert disproportionate economic (and often political) hold on LDCs and the independence of their economies.

(i) *On the production of capital goods*

Mass poverty and low income levels for the majority in the LDCs mean that these countries tend not to have levels of consumer demand high enough to develop their own autonomous capital goods industries, that is heavy goods and machine-producing industries. Thus it is not surprising to find, as we have noted, that those industries which have developed in the countries of the South tend to be those producing simple consumer goods or else raw materials for export. This would not be a cause for concern if technologies were widely available to LDCs at low cost and in forms readily adaptable to an integrated development strategy oriented to labour-surplus economies. But in practice, most available technology originates in the West and is available from western-based TNCs mostly in a 'packaged' form rather than in separate components. Tight control of patents, a high concentration of research and development in the labour-scarce northern economies and high royalty payments all work against LDCs trying to learn from and adapt technologies for their own use. Furthermore, many aid transfers from rich to poor countries are often conditional upon recipient countries purchasing equipment from donor countries, usually little adapted to the needs of the majority in the host countries. Thus it is not surprising to find that the sophisticated technology on offer and supplied to LDCs, particularly that used by the TNCs in their Third World operations, is usually only available to the top 10 to 20 per cent of the population who are wealthy enough either to purchase it or to purchase the more luxurious consumer goods made from it. The need that LDCs have to trade with the North and the dominance that TNCs have in world trade tends also to lead to the displacement of traditional technologies and their replacement by modern western-supplied technologies, just as traditionally-produced products are often replaced by the shiny, expensively-packaged TNC-produced goods. The power that TNCs have on Third World countries through their technologies is particularly severe in the most dynamic sectors of the economy; these are often oriented to export with the products made to international specifications. The result is often that integration with the North is strengthened at the cost of dislocation within LDC economies.

(ii) *On employment*

The employment effects of TNC operations within the Third World also tend to reinforce North-South links and to strengthen global and intra-LDC inequalities. Although TNCs do provide Third World nations with jobs, they tend on the one hand to produce relatively few high paid jobs and with wage levels equated more with similar jobs paid by the corporations world-wide than with other incomes in the host country. Except under pressure, TNCs have tended to be slow in training local personnel for these skilled jobs and the régime of internationally-comparable pay levels works against any national wages and incomes policies oriented to a redistribution in favour of poorer groups.

On the other hand, TNCs have traditionally provided most of their jobs to low-paid labour, often engaged in repetitive jobs. Indeed, TNCs have often been attracted to the South because of the low wages they can pay in relation to comparable jobs in the North. Within six years of the first move overseas by a United States' semi-conductor firm, all major producers had located their assembly operations in low labour-cost economies. While these operations undoubtedly do provide jobs in economies with huge unemployment problems, as host countries have no control over world-wide location of TNC operations and, as we have seen, are given little opportunity to acquire and adapt technologies used in the whole production process, there is no guarantee that long-term employment will be achieved. When the TNC decides to relocate elsewhere, employment will be lost. It is no accident that TNCs have been attracted to and welcomed by national security states in Latin America, southern Africa and the Far East and by countries which have consistently flouted the rights of workers, particularly of the low-paid, as the experience of Brazil, South Africa and South Korea clearly indicates.

(iii) *On national sovereignty*

This brings us to another area of concern over the operations of TNCs in the Third World, namely the challenge they bring to national sovereignty. Of the hundred largest economic units in the world today, only half are nation States; the other half are TNCs. The annual turnover of the United States corporation General Motors is higher than the national income of over 50 LDCs. In 1976, the total sales of foreign affiliates of western TNCs totalled US$860 billion, exceeding the total national income of all non-oil-exporting countries of the South.

This ecomonic power which TNCs have acquired, particularly in the last 3 decades, has led some of them to use this power both to enter directly into political activity and also to be able to avoid taxes and other payments. In 1977, it was estimated that TNCs paid out between them a staggering US$350 million in illegal or questionable payments including sums for bribery and extortion. Some TNCs have engaged in vigorous transfer pricing—the procedure of lowering prices in high tax régimes and raising them in lower tax régimes for different parts of the production process which is carried out in different countries—thereby reducing the overall tax burden and decreasing the revenue of particular LDCs. This type of activity has, in effect, enabled TNCs to establish their own international currency exchange rates and so lead to the further erosion of national control. In recent years, too, evidence has come to light of TNCs earning super-profits often as high as 600 per cent. This, together with the practice by some corporations of 'dumping' products banned or considered dangerous by governments of the North onto Third World consumers has contributed to the direct exploitation of the poor by the rich and the excess profits could be seen as a kind of subsidy to consumers within the industrialised nations.

(d) Further deterioration through the micro-electronics revolution

The advent of the micro-electronics revolution and the increasing use being made of the silicon chip in many varied processes of production will add yet more problems for the South. The coming widespread use of micro-electronics is likely to erode what comparative advantage many Third World countries have over western industrialised countries, namely a plentiful supply of low-cost labour. Already in both the garment industry and on car assembly lines, robots are taking over repetitive labour-intensive operations and as this practice develops it is expected that TNCs will begin to relocate their industries in their home countries. Not only will this make it harder for LDCs to promote their own programmes of industrialisation, where such technology is utilised in LDCs, but Third World dependency on the North and on TNCs in particular will increase yet further because micro-electronic technology is even more difficult to unpackage than more traditional types of technology.

3. THE NEED FOR FUNDAMENTAL REFORM

As we noted at the start of this article, the present world economic system has resulted in an increase in international inequalities, and where growth has occurred in the Third World it has tended not to benefit the poorest sectors of the population. In so far as TNCs play an important, increasingly and largely unregulated role in reinforcing North-South economic relations, their activities can be considered a major cause of present problems. (One should add, however, that the possibility, and even the probability, of exceptions remains.) This suggests, at the very least, that strict controls over the operations of TNCs and the provision of mechanisms of public accountability should become a major priority for those concerned with poverty, unemployment and income redistribution in the Third World.

Although many of the problems which TNCs pose for Third World countries are readily admitted, the claim is often made, however, that investment in these countries by foreign capital in general and by TNCs in particular is the surest way of achieving high rates of economic growth, the benefits of which could then be redistributed throughout the economy. While this may be true for certain countries at particular stages of development, recent historical evidence suggests the following:

> redistribution and secondary transfers are ineffective means of correcting primary inequality associated with the ownership of productive assets, whether these are physical assets or human capital. Once growth is taking place and incomes are earned, it is difficult to redistribute incomes by means of taxes, public employment and the like.[3]

But even more disturbing for the present world economic order is recent evidence which goes even further to suggest that although private capital investment and aid do contribute to short run benefits for a country's balance of payments, the structural effects of large stocks of foreign capital are not only detrimental to income redistribution, but also *reduce growth*. A recent review of 16 independent studies on economic growth and inequality conducted over the past 10 years came to the following conclusions:

> The effect of direct foreign investment and foreign aid has been to increase income inequality within countries. This effect holds for income inequality, land inequality and sectoral income inequality. Flows of direct foreign investment and foreign aid have had a short-term effect of increasing the relative rate of economic growth of countries. Stocks of direct investment and foreign aid have had the cumulative effect of decreasing the relative rate of economic growth of countries. This effect is small in the short run (1-5 years) and gets larger in the long run (5-20 years).[4]

Of course this evidence does not necessarily point to recommendations that LDCs should now stop aid and investment flows into their economies: the second state could be worse than the first and other negative results could arise. Furthermore, the effect of TNCs within LDCs and on the world economy are only part of much wider problems. Other important factors which need to be analysed include trade in commodities and other trade arrangements, access and distribution of energy resources, the world monetary system, the operations of international financial institutions and the whole question of arms sales. But this article does point to the urgent need for fundamental reforms in the world system in general and in the operation of TNCs in particular.

4. THE END OF THE ORDER—THE BEGINNING OF ANOTHER?

As the decade of the 1980s begins, western industrialised economies are faced with a number of critical problems: international recession, increasing levels of unemployment not seen since the 1930s' Depression, high rates of inflation and escalating oil prices. In this context of international economic gloom, it is only too easy to be led to believe that the central problem lies in inefficiencies in the present world economic system and that what is needed is another period of economic expansion, as experienced in the 3 decades following World War II. This article has shown such an approach to be totally misguided. What is needed and what representatives of the poor countries are demanding with growing vehemence is a new restructured world economy. As the Secretary-General of the United Nations Conference on Trade and Development (UNCTAD) stressed recently:

> "The compelling need for a new order is not based on the consideration that the prevailing order is no longer working well. It is based on the more fundamental premise that the prevailing order did not satisfy . . . (the) needs (of the South) even when it was working best."[5]

Notes

1. Address to the Second United Nations Conference on Trade and Development, Santiago, Chile, 14 April 1972.
2. *North-South: A Programme for Survival*, The Report of the Independent Commission on International Development Issues under the Chairmanship of Willy Brandt (London 1980) p. 32.
3. United Nations Industrial Development Organisation (UNIDO) *World Industry since 1960: Progress and Prospects* (New York 1979) p. 248.
4. V. Bornschier, C. Chase-Dunn and R. Rubinson, 'Cross-national evidence of the effects of foreign investment and aid on economic growth and inequality; a survey of findings and a reanalysis' *American Journal of Sociology* (1978) pp. 651-683.
5. United Nations Conference on Trade and Development (UNCTAD) *New Directions and New Structures for Trade and Development* (Geneva 1976) section 3, paragraph 7.

PART II

On the Theory of the North-South Conflict

Vincent Cosmao

The Ideology of National Security

1. THE DECLARATIONS OF PUEBLA ABOUT THE IDEOLOGY OF NATIONAL SECURITY

ONE OF the issues at stake at the Third General Assembly of the Latin American Episcopate (Puebla, 27 January-13 February 1979) was the definition of the Church's position with regard to the doctrine, or the ideology, of national security. Invoking a 'subjective profession of the Christian faith' (no. 49)* or claiming to be 'defending western Christian civilisation' (no. 547), some, at least, of the champions of this ideology did, indeed, consider it to be self-evident that their struggle should be legitimised by a Church whose traditional function has been to administer the social myths, rites, language and systems of values of the various Latin American countries.

Acting prudently[1] but firmly, the Conference refused to be persuaded by this view, preserving its independence from the ideology of national security as well as from 'liberal capitalism' and 'Marxist collectivism'. This ideology was criticised as being 'totalitarian' and 'authoritarian', and therefore as leading to the violation of human rights (no. 49); as being 'statist', organising the whole life of society for a 'total war' against the menace of communism and therefore limiting, by this very fact, individual liberties (no. 314); as being 'élitist' and 'verticalist' and thereby restricting popular participation in political decision-making (no. 547). The attribution of absolute value to national security and to the State which is responsible for it was presented as an 'institutionalisation of individual insecurity' (no. 314).

These declarations, which reveal the beginnings of a consensus, are the culmination of a long process of growing awareness by the Church of the political trends which have been taking shape in Latin America. Having at first welcomed the intervention of the armed forces as a protection against disorder, anarchy or communism, the episcopate, in one country after another, was to be confronted by violations of human rights which turned out to be no mere accidents on the way to the restoration of the social order which it recognised as necessary. Since liberalism, rationalist and positivist, had seriously weakened the colonial version of Christendom, and socialism had undermined from its inception the new, 'populist' Christendom, another return to Christendom under the protection of the armed forces became, thenceforth, difficult to imagine.[2]

* The numbers in brackets refer to the final document issued by the Puebla Conference. Official edition, CELAM, 1979, 284 pp.

Even the 'corrective' legitimisation of the régimes which had come to power by these methods was gradually to be ruled out, although it would probably have been preferred by the dominant element of the ecclesiastical establishment. The spread of the 'social doctrine of the Church', Catholic Action, the influence of such men as Maritain, Mounier, Lebret, etc., had, since the Thirties, created among the clerical and lay élite a state of mind which made such an alliance between Church and State unlikely. Thus the age of a transplanted form of Christendom which might have survived its disappearance in Europe drew to a close.

2. THE ORIGIN AND CONTENT OF THE IDEOLOGY OF NATIONAL SECURITY

The defenders of order claimed, however, to be the defenders of the 'free world' under the aegis of its leader, the USA. In the same period the international debate on human rights had not succeeded in establishing an effective relationship between the defence of 'liberty' and of the needs of organised social life, or 'order'. Following 'liberal' and 'social' traditions the debate produced, in 1966, two international pacts, one concerning 'civil and political rights', the other 'economic, social and cultural rights', having failed to achieve a synthesis between the two categories.

The doctrine of national security appears historically as a by-product of this debate, in which the attribution of an absolute status to 'order' becomes the necessary condition for the maintenance of a system of which the 'liberties' constitute the practical and theoretical frame of reference. Thus, resistance to an actual totalitarianism led to the creation of a doctrinal totalitarianism.

From 1968, in Brazil, a group of experts co-ordinated by Dom Padin, at that time Bishop of Lorena, now Bishop of Bauru, embarked on a critical analysis of the doctrine of national security, based on official documents of the Brazilian régime and on a book by one of the theoreticians of the new policy, General Golberry do Couto e Silva.[3] This study showed clearly how in the 'total war' between the 'Christian, democratic West' and the 'materialist, communist East', the State, being responsible for the nation, has absolute power to mobilise and plan the life of the community, imposing all the sacrifices it deems necessary for the general interest or the common good. Moreover, the armed forces, the élite of the nation, are alone qualified to lead the State. Christianity, 'the supreme standard for social life', should furnish the language necessary to inculcate in the population submission to the demands of this total and permanent war.

Since that time critics have stressed the North American or 'Pan-Germanist' inspiration of this political philosophy which was elaborated most forcefully at the beginning of the Cold War and during the wars fought by France in Indo-China and Algeria.[4] Thus one can see more clearly how the siege-mentality produces a polarisation on 'the enemy' which leads one to identify with the image which one has formed of that enemy. From this point of view the doctrine of national security appears as the culmination of the East-West confrontation in its ideological dimension.

But the 'salvaging' of Christianity as the ideological framework for the indoctrination and mobilisation of the masses leads also to the attempt to interpret this doctrine as the (final) incarnation of Christendom. Those things which are really at stake in Christianity as an historical movement might then appear more clearly, and the Church would find itself compelled to redefine the essential basis of the practice of its faith with reference to the organisation of the life of the community, on the level of individual societies and on that of the world society which must be constructed.

3. INQUIRING INTO THE POLITICAL FUNCTION OF CHRISTIANITY

However much one tries to minimise its political significance, conscious or unconscious, early Christianity had to take up a position in relation to the civil power, specifically in relation to the power of Caesar. In the argument over taxation,[5] the basic position of Jesus is contained in what he leaves unsaid: to render to God what belongs to God, that is, worship, means, obviously, that one refuses to worship Caesar, because God alone is God, or because there is no other god but God. But the attribution of sacred status to the system, which was one based on colonisation and slavery, was necessary for the levying of taxes. On this basis the first generations of Christians could compromise on the question of submission to the authorities and on the whole social and political organisation, including slavery; they may have spoken the language of obedience, but in practice, nonetheless, they were dissidents as soon as the issue of worship arose. The martyrs who refused to bow down before the idol were denying in practice the sacredness of the social system, which was equivalent to stating that God alone is God, and 'Jesus whom He has made Lord'. This profession of faith was, albeit in a 'clandestine' manner, radically opposed to the raising of the civil power to a sacred or absolute level. It implied moreover that this power should merely be an instrument in the service of the life of the community. 'The kings of the gentiles exercise lordship over them; and those in authority over them are called benefactors (a title with religious connotations). But not so with you; rather let the greatest among you become as the youngest, and the leader as one who serves . . .'.[6] The political significance of these words, which have been generally interpreted as idealistic or moralistic, has been too much underestimated. The involvement of religion in the necessary organisation of communal life is henceforth challenged: politics is thus reduced to its proper function which is to be the practical means of structuring social relationships and of building societies; it is made the responsibility of the citizens themselves, since the Judeo-Christian tradition offers no other norm than that of resistance to social structures based on inequality, and to the injustice which that inequality produces when as a result some people lack the necessities of life (Matt. 25).

These obvious facts, which hardly needed to be made explicit since they had such a decisive effect on practice, began to be less in evidence once the Emperor, 'becoming a Christian', was seen as God's lieutenant, and when, in addition, with the dissolution of the eastern Empire, the Church was obliged to accord him sacred status to ensure the continued functioning of the social structure. Over the centuries the relationship and the rivalry between pope and emperor, between clergy and nobility, would inevitably cause Christianity to be used to legitimise, to control and to give sacred authority to the structures of society, so that it was transformed into the 'civil religion' of the West, with the advantages and disadvantages that this entailed. There were disadvantages in so far as the interpretation of Christianity in relation to God and to the conduct of the affairs of this world was concerned. Whereas the recognition of God as Creator of man in his image and likeness led to the collective responsibility of man in directing his own history, the criterion being the possibility of life for all, the delegation of all power to a few, who were considered to have a mandate from God, was to become the norm, in a 'hierarchy' distinguishing 'those who pray', 'those who fight' and 'those who work', these 'three orders' (Duby) apparently springing from the 'three functions' (Dumézil) of the Indo-European tradition.

Whatever may have been the undeniable achievements of this Christendom, it may nevertheless be seen, when it is analysed, as the 'perversion' of Christianity through having been made an instrument in the service of the social order. 'Modernism' has emerged from the need to criticise the 'régimes' which had thus been immutably established 'for all eternity' because of their sacred character. Even in its development into atheism it remains faithful to the logic of primitive Christianity, or at least it forces Christianity to rediscover the truth, both practical and theoretical, of its origins. At that point, the bestowal of sacred status on the structures of society was precluded because of the obvious fact that there is no other god than God, or that there is nothing 'divine' in social hierarchies. From this point of view, primitive Christianity was, in effect, a subversive force seeking the recognition of God alone as God.

The fact that 'eternal life', in the eschatological sense of the term, was not the only horizon by which the faith was bounded, since the criterion of the truth of that faith was the obligation to feed the hungry and therefore to organise the community in such a way as to ensure that no-one should lack the necessities of life, is more difficult to demonstrate, since the understanding of the Word of God has been so much determined by the practice of hundreds of years of Christendom. When the social order was considered sacred, 'resignation' was the only possibility allowed to those who had to submit to it, even if that order condemned them to die through not receiving their share of the resources available. This identification of religion with resignation was an obvious corollary of the sacred status accorded to the unequal organisation of society, even if it does not correspond to the dynamic of Christianity.

4. THE NEW 'CHRISTENDOM' OF THE INDUSTRIAL SYSTEM AND CHRISTIANITY AS A LIBERATING FORCE

In the industrialised countries which have sprung from Christendom it is the criticism 'from the outside' of that Christendom which has progressively destroyed it, leading Christianity, amid its nostalgia and its dreams of 'restoration', to rethink its own nature, both in terms of a 'return to its origins' and from the standpoint of 'eternal life', even if in practice it was involving itself in politics, often, moreover, with an eye to a return to Christendom. The maintenance of the faith in the face of unbelief had a more decisive importance, in theology, than the practice of the faith in history, in the construction of societies. As a result Christianity, or the Church, has appeared to have only marginal importance as a social force, even if culture and language are still strongly marked by its imprint.

In Latin America events did not follow the same pattern. After the positivist 'digression' of the nineteenth century, the structure of Christendom re-emerged unscathed within the social structure, and the reorganisation of the Church, stimulated by the influences coming from Europe, made it possible to think of its restoration. Within the logic of the Cold War, the mobilisation of the masses, with the collaboration of the Church, for an anti-communist 'crusade' could not be ruled out. Latin America appeared even at the end of the Fifties as the ideal hinterland for such an enterprise. Christendom provided a 'structure' in which the resignation of the poor and therefore their submission to the authorities constituted the most significant element.

The aim of the upholders of the doctrine of national security was less a total and permanent war against international communism or the 'defence of the free world' than the modernisation of the machinery of production and the integration of the sub-continent into the industrial system, whatever the social and human cost. The outward-looking 'model of development' which most of the countries ruled by 'strong' régimes have attempted to put into operation reveals clearly that the resignation of the poor was the 'temporary' condition of economic growth; increased production had to precede any redistribution of incomes: the maintenance of order was necessary for such a policy.

The growing influence of Marxism made this method of running the economy, with the direct result of relegating an increasingly high percentage of the population to a marginal or sub-proletarian status, very hazardous. The denunciation of the atheism of the Marxists would therefore mobilise the Church on the side of the defenders of 'western Christian civilisation', a by-product of that Christendom whose restoration was still not unthinkable.

If this story is far from being over it seems very likely that its coherence has been weakened, less as a result of the involvement of the Church in the defence of human rights—the effects of this involvement are not always obvious, since the concern for order leads inevitably to the relativisation of liberties—than because of the current changes which are taking place in the understanding of Christianity and in the Church's practice of the faith. It is the poor who are becoming aware that resignation is not 'true religion': hearing the Good News which is once more being proclaimed to them, and which they are proclaiming in their turn, they are mobilising for their own liberation, denouncing as an 'atheist the man who oppresses his brother'. Refusing a 'religious' submission to the order which men have sought to impose on them as sacred, they are rediscovering 'instinctively' the original dynamic of Christianity: they are organising themselves to ensure that no-one will lack the necessities of life, and they are ready to die rather than submit to an order which they see as contradicting the divine purpose whose first requirement is that all may live.

Thus we see 'unmasked' the real lines of force of the ideology of national security: the point towards a 'development' seen as the reproduction of the industrial model and an integration into the multinational capitalist system, without taking any account of the 'essential needs' of their people. Unlike the 'primitive capitalism' of the beginning of the industrial era, political practice is here underpinned by a doctrine, a theory or an ideology of that 'smiling future' in the name of which the present generation is called upon to sacrifice itself with the prospect of paradise as a recompense.

By recovering its place in history, with its demands that the life of the community should be organised in such a way that no man goes short of what he needs, Christianity is becoming once more the movement of resistance and liberation which it was, at least potentially, before it lost its identity in Christendom. In the future it is not its 'contamination' by Marxism which should cause apprehension, for the rebirth of Christianity as an historical movement is more to be feared by those régimes which feel an anxious need to achieve a sacred status than is any other movement which does not take account of its relationship to God as imposing the requirement that man should be responsible for encouraging the progress and the creation of his fellow man, and as rejecting any form of social organisation whose primary objective is not to ensure the possibility of life for all.

Translated by L. H. Ginn

Notes

1. In the index of the official version of the Puebla Document the term 'national security' refers, rather curiously, to sections which recognise the necessity of national security for every political organisation; it is the term '*doctrine* of national security' which refers to those pages in which this doctrine is denounced.

2. P. Richard *Mord des Chrétientés et naissance de l'Eglise*, an historical analysis and theological interpretation of the Church in Latin America (Paris 1978) 235 pp. offset.

3. 'A doctrina da Segurança Nacional a Luz da Doctrina da Ingréja' *Sedoc*/especial, set. 1968, 432-444. The central section of this article has been translated into French in *DIAL* (170 bvd de Monparnasse, 75014 Paris), no. 302, 6 May 1976. The first edition of the book by General Golberry, *Geopolitica do Brasil*, appeared in 1966, (São Paulo); 2nd edition 1967, 266 pp. *DIAL* has also published, in 1976, no. 298, 15 April, an anonymous article written in Chile in 1975.

4. J. Comblin *Le Pouvoir militair en Amérique latine: l'idéologie de la Sécurité nationale* (Paris 1977) 229 pp.

5. Matt. 22:15-22, Mark 12:13-17, Luke 20:20-26.

6. Luke 22:25-27.

Pieter Verloren van Themaat

The Legal Foundations of a New International Economic Order

1. WHY THE DEMAND FOR A NEW INTERNATIONAL ECONOMIC ORDER?

TO FIND an objective explanation for this demand one has to take account of 3 separate historical developments.

The first and most important development is the fact that after World War II many western colonies acquired independence. This led to the creation of a great number of new independent States. On the one hand these new States were determined to have their recently acquired sovereignty treated as on the same level with the older States (the principle of equality of sovereignty). On the other hand these developing countries became increasingly convinced that their inferior state of development and the frequently even absolute poverty of their peoples were the result of the way in which the 'old' international economic order operated. And particularly when the oil-exporting developing countries had demonstrated their economic, and with it, their political potential, these developing countries began to attack the prevailing international economic order (OPEC). This led in 1974 to the three well-known Resolutions of the United Nations (3201, 3202 and 3281) on the Establishment of a New International Economic Order (NIEO), the Programme of Action on this New International Economic Order and the Charter of Economic Rights and Duties of States.

Secondly, 1972 saw the publication of *The limits to growth*, the first report brought out for the members of the Club of Rome. This made many western politicians realise that a vast number of world-wide interdependent problems were bound to affect western prosperity sooner or later as much as the rest of the world. Moreover, it would be impossible to find a solution for these problems without much further progress in international co-operation.

These problems were: the growth of the world-population, how to provide the raw materials, energy and food which this growing population would need, the protection of the natural environment, the international legal machinery necessary to control the exploitation of the natural resources of the sea, the sea-bed and ocean floor, and subsoil thereof, the fact that even western countries are unable to exercise any effective control over transnational and multinational enterprises and international cartels (the question of restrictive business practices), and finally, the need for a much better co-ordination of the many international interventions which would become imperative in the problem areas just mentioned and those that have already been identified for some years.

The most important areas where international co-operation has already been working for some time are: the regulation of international trade and commerce (GATT and UNCTAD), the adjustment and harmonisation of the international monetary system (IMF), and the organisation of financial and technical assistance to developing countries (World Bank, UNDP and regional Development Banks). Since the Sixties the whole complexity of the problems of the developing countries was already being tackled by the United Nations in its international development strategy by means of its more or less structured development decades. The third decade is due this year, 1980.

So we come to the third strand in this historical development.

When the energy crisis exploded in 1973 modern western welfare States brought out a whole crop of protective measures which led obviously to increasing national tensions within such already existing international economic bodies as GATT, IMF, the EEC, and the OECD.

The drift towards protectionism, backed by new ways of pursuing it in practice, obviously meant that the old rules by which the western countries played their international trade game, had to be revised and broadened.

The international monetary system simply has to function in a way which takes account of the various national economic intervention policies. These policies are obviously concerned with inflation, unemployment and the balance of payment deficits which result from the energy crisis.

From the structural point of view, this whole third strand implies that we can no longer blindly cling to the initial post-war idea of achieving an international redistribution of goods, services and productivity by interfering as little as possible with the international market forces.

The international economic order will simply have to accept that we have to move towards a 'mixed economic order', just as most western countries have had to accept this fact of life. But this means that the economic system can no longer be run simply on the so-called 'free' lines of uninhibited supply and demand, but has also to be governed by clearly stated national and international interventions.

2. CONTINUITY AND CHANGE IN THE LEGAL FOUNDATIONS OF THE INTERNATIONAL ECONOMIC ORDER

International economic law is developing in two ways: by way of continuity and by way of gradually accelerating change.

The line of continuity goes back historically to the treaties which Italian city-states concluded with Arabian princes and Hansa cities in N.W. Europe in the twelfth and thirteenth centuries. It is curious to find Arabian princes at the beginning of both the old international economic order and the new one.

Some principles concerning equality in the world of commerce go back to the beginning of the old order. Thus, for instance, the principle of reciprocity when certain commercial benefits are granted; or the principle of parity by which foreign merchants are entitled to the same treatment as nationals, and the 'most-favoured-nation' principle. This last is really a clause which means that the parties to a treaty are automatically entitled to such more favourable trading conditions as one of the two parties has granted to a third party.

These 3 principles, aimed at a relatively free trade, are still standard ingredients of international treaties, and it is remarkable that, from the twelfth century on, they have remained an integral part of the legal basis of international business.

The first and third principles are mentioned explicitly in GATT and the second in the Rome Treaty of the EEC.

In the course of the centuries they were obviously worked out in greater detail and precision.

The initial trend towards free trade was emphasised during this period and reached new peaks in the second half of the nineteenth and the second half of the twentieth centuries. During these centuries 4 other basic norms came to be added to the original 3.

There was the principle of the 'open door', meaning that all foreign nations had equal commercial opportunities in regions still dependent on one country; the principle of preferential treatment, which applies to countries with which one party to a treaty has some specific relationship or countries which find themselves in a peculiar situation; the principle of equity; and lastly, the 'minimal' norm which is important for countries where national law provides no real satisfactory solution for foreigners.

Although these 4 later norms arrived on the scene rather late, with the exception of the 'open door' principle, they play an important part in today's international economic law.

Because Schwarzenberger was one of the first to define these standard principles, people have taken to speaking of the 'seven standards of Schwarzenberger'. If you look for them, you can find them all incorporated in the Charter of Economic Rights and Duties of States.

This means that they are still felt to be the basis of the new international economic order pursued today. In other words, we are still clinging to the traditional 'continuity'.

The 'gradually accelerating change', mentioned above, emerged in various ways.

First of all, as already observed, there is the continuing process of elaborating in greater detail the 7 principles which still form the basis.

Second, there was a flowering of bilateral and multilateral treaties and international organisations since the last quarter of the last century.

The nineteenth century produced these international organisations mainly in such areas of technological development as post and telegraph. After World War II there was a vast increase in international organisations, but this time it was in the field of economics—and they are still growing.

This particular article is based on extensive investigations mainly concerned with examining the experience of these international economic organisations from the angle of comparative law.

The third and by far the most important change in international mercantile law since the twelfth century came about as follows.

The rise of these international economic organisations not only stressed the principles of 'freedom' (particularly in commerce and the transfer of payments, but also linked with other productivity factors) and a sort of formal equality, but added to this principles of material equality, such as equal competition, including States or ethnic groups that are economically weak. But these international organisations also show an increasing number of variants on the principle of solidarity.

These variants of the new principle of solidarity are very relevant today. They oblige each State to take account in its own domestic policies of the interests of other countries, to inform and consult these other countries, to assist each other financially, technologically and juridically. And in an increasing number of cases this principle even binds States to co-operate together to the degree of handing over certain powers until the international organisations have agreed on settling the matter with regard to some specific projects.

As is understandable, it is precisely these obligations implied in the principle of solidarity which are predominant in the Charter of the economic rights and duties of States.

There they are most developed with regard to the exploitation of the ocean floor and its subsoil as well as in matters concerning the natural environment. These 2 issues have been declared to concern the common heritage of mankind and are thus a matter of the common responsibility of all mankind.

Apart from this, the IMF, the World Bank, the Agreements on raw materials, the regional organisations of the West (e.g., the EEC), the regional organisations of developing countries (e.g., the Andes group and until recently the East African Community) can all lead to a high degree of 'supra-nationalism'. The economic Charter also recognises this potential trend towards supra-national features, sometimes explicitly and sometimes by implication. Indications of this supra-national development are the degree to which certain sectors of international organisations can operate independently of national governments, as well as the degree to which decisions taken by international organisations can be directly binding on member States or their citizens. Although the Charter has no coercive force in law and certain western countries expressed some reservations, it was nevertheless meant to lay down the main legal foundations of a new international economic order.

3. THE LEGAL BASIS OF A NEW INTERNATIONAL ECONOMIC ORDER AND ETHIC

Legal principles which can be brought together under such more comprehensive principles as freedom, equality and solidarity may easily give the impression that they are based on moral principles.

It is true that among those who in the western and in developing countries stand for a new international economic order, many are motivated by moral principles. I myself have quoted examples of this in my book with the same title as this article. Nevertheless there is a danger here which has to be mentioned.

Historically speaking one is no doubt on firmer ground when seeing enlightened economic self-interest as the basis of such legal principles. The same holds for the principle of solidarity. This seems to have sprung from the realisation that we live in a situation of economic interdependence.

Then we have the fact that western authors like Röling and spokesmen for the Third World like Abí-Saab have drawn attention to the profound mistrust evinced by the developing countries towards the western nations who, while parading as Christian, or, later on, humanist, or simply civilised, in practice pursued for centuries a policy of political, military and finally economic domination. This mistrust extends even to the Universal Declaration of Human Rights and the various Conventions linked with it.

Individual people actively involved in the re-structuring of the international economic order may certainly be acting on a moral conviction rooted in Christianity, some other religion or plain humanism. But because of their centuries-old painful experience of western morality in actual practice, one can hardly blame the developing countries when they prefer this re-structuring to be based on mutual economic interest, the acquisition of more know-how, strengthening their own power and hoping to achieve as high a degree of self-reliance as possible.

As has already been suggested, the history of international economic law in the western countries or, for that matter, those countries where the economy is State-controlled, does not show any great worries about ethics.

Finally, one cannot overlook that the proper matter of moral norms is interpersonal (individual or collective) relationships. Now, from the juridical point of view the most important declaration of principles with regard to the NIEO is the economic Charter.

But this Charter deals exclusively with the rights and duties of States. So far any attempt to insert guarantees for the recognition of human rights into the framework of economic co-operation has always failed. This was still the case as recently as the negotiations about the second Lomé treaty which dealt with the economic co-operation between the European Community and 57 developing countries. Moreover, such attempts are sometimes seen as interfering with the internal affairs of a country and thus in conflict with the principle of sovereignty which is recognised in the Charter.

Anyway, this principle of sovereignty and the non-consideration of the individual rights and obligations of subjects, including enterprises, constitute a weakness in the Charter, not merely from the ethical, but also from the rational and juridical point of view. When, for instance, a major power introduces a restrictive budget, or pursues a particular policy in industry or agriculture, this may have severe effects on the economic development of other countries.

It is therefore important for the developing countries that, in a new international economic order, international co-operation should include some real hold on the internal economic policies of the member States. This is not sufficiently recognised in the Charter.

Moreover, there will never be any effective control over multinational enterprises and international cartels if there are no international norms for business which are binding and can be internationally enforced. I have found abundant evidence for this statement in my own experience when working for the EEC.

Finally, it is impossible to overcome the absolute poverty of hundreds of millions of people in developing countries until it is internationally recognised that they have a *right* to have their basic needs provided for by effective measures taken at national and international level. This right postulates an international *obligation* to lay down corresponding national measures, as well as international measures to support the national ones. People cannot live on charity alone. And here again, enlightened political and economic motivation can provide a sound foundation for such rights and obligations.

Does this mean that the Churches have no contribution to make to the NIEO? Of course not. To start with, they can strengthen rationally motivated objectives by moral support and actual fieldwork. The most poignant reproach addressed by the developing countries to the developed ones is that, in the world at large, the developed countries refuse to apply to developing countries the kind of machinery which they themselves have discovered and applied to achieve some of their most noble objectives (the Yugoslav jurist Blagojević, Manley and Ramphal). Here the developing countries compare the rational and moral basis for many western social, regional and agricultural policies and their own 'development' policies (in the broad sense), with the ways in which they control the world market in the matter of raw materials.

In actual fact, a much more just international economic order would not ask much more than that the 'development' policies, pursued within and between the developed countries, particularly after World War II, should be applied much more widely.

Even here, enlightened economic considerations, a greater sharing of knowledge and the growing economic power of 'weaker' countries have often clinched the matter whatever the moral arguments. In all probability, the achievement of an NIEO will run on the same lines.

In spite of all this, one finds that there are still deeper reasons why moral theology, religious sociology and cultural anthropology should be more involved in this matter of an NIEO.

To start with, any legal principle will have to be tested in all the divergent cultures by the prevailing outlook on life and the world at large.

Moreover, our study has made it clear that, in the end, whatever we say, there are certain basic options of which any NIEO will have to take note, which simply cannot be reduced to purely rational economic considerations.

Thus in countries with a State-controlled economy the individual freedoms of people and enterprises are made to serve the interests of the community while in western countries (even in their understanding of international economic co-operation) the principle of equality and that of solidarity are ultimately subjected to the right of people, enterprises and nations to take decisions which suit themselves: the right of self-determination.

Abbreviations

EEC: The European Economic Community of nine West-European countries working together. This is the most important Community, along with the EC for Coal and Steel, and the EC for Atomic Energy.

GATT: General Agreement on Tariffs and Trade, and the corresponding organisation to which 84 States belong.

IMF: International Monetary Fund.

NIEO: The New International Economic Order.

OECD: The Organisation for Economic Co-operation and Development. This brings together the industrialised countries which have an economic system mainly dominated by the free market forces of capitalism.

UNCTAD: United Nations Conference on Trade and Development, set up by the UN Economic and Social Council (ECOSOC) which is rather dominated by the developing countries, in which it differs from GATT, the IMF and the World Bank.

UNDP: The United Nations Development Programme, an organisation which plays a prominent role in equipping the developing countries for the introduction of technological projects.

Translated by Theo Westow

Bibliography

Saab, J. Abí 'The third world and the future of the international legal order' *Revue égyptienne de droit international* (1973) 27-66.

Bergsten, C. F., ed. *The Future of the International Economic Order: an agenda for research* (Lexington (Mass.)/Toronto/London 1973).

Blagojević, B. T. 'Quelques caractéristiques du droit économique international actuel' *Revue internationale de droit comparé* (1968) 207-273.

Kapteyn, P. J. G. *De verenigde Naties en de internationale economische ordre* (containing the complete texts of the most important UN resolutions in NIEO), part of the series edited by P. Verloren van Themaat: *Studies over internationaal economisch recht* (The Hague and Alphen a.d. Rijn 1977) I.1. Vols. I.2-I.5 of this series examine in detail the other most important international economic organisations from the legal point of view and various problematic areas in some 28 specified studies.

Manley, M. 'Parallels of equity. New horizons in economic co-operation' *Round Table* (1975) 335-347.

Meadows, D. H., Meadows, D. L., Randers, J., Behrens, W. *The Limits to Growth* (New York 1972).

Ramphal, S. S. 'The other world in this one: the promise of the new international economic order' *Round Table* (1976) 61-72.

Röling, B. V. A. *International law in an Expanded World* (Amsterdam 1960).

Schwarzenberger, G. 'Standards of International Economic Law' *The International Law Quarterly* (1948) 405 ff.

Tinbergen, J., co-ord. *Reshaping the international order* (New York 1976).

Verloren van Themaat, P. *Economic law of the Member States of the European Community in an Economic and Monetary Union* (Brussels 1973) (Commission of the European Communities, Studies, Competition—Approximation of legislation series).

Verloren van Themaat, P. *Rechtsgrondslagen van een nieuwe internationale economische ordre. Studies over internationaal economisch recht*, Pt. II (The Hague/Alphen a.d. Rijn 1979), with further literature from all parts of the world (English edition to appear in 1980 under the title of *The Changing Structure of International Economic Law*).

Verloren van Themaat, P. 'Quelques réflexions sur les méthodes d'intégration en Europe occidentale et en Europe orientale' *Mélanges Fernand Dehousse* (Liège 1979) 95-100.

Georges Enderle and Ambros Lüthi

Economic Dependence and Dissociation

1. INTRODUCTION

DEPENDENCE can occur in the internal and external economic spheres. It means that the country, region or class in question is not economically autonomous; that is, economic activities in trade and production cannot be determined in essentials by the corresponding social entities, but are imposed from without. This introduces 2 modes of conceptual demarcation. Dependence is an asymmetrical relationship and is not to be confused with interdependence which consists of symmetrical relations of 'partnership' between 2 or more autonomous economic entities. Autonomy, moreover, does not mean autarky which may be defined as the absence of any external relationships.

Since World War II several countries have achieved political independence. Therefore we have to ask whether and how far this independence has also been realised in the economic sphere, and what are the effects of economic dependence on the development process in the Third World. This complex of problems has been studied by many sociologists, economists and politologists in all continents.[1]

2. THE DEPENDENCIA SCHOOL

Properly speaking the theory of dependence, the *dependencia* school, which is not of course a closed theoretical system, originated in Latin America. The analyses of dependence, which had a decisive influence on the social sciences in Latin America and elsewhere and were often associated with political campaigns, arose from a complex of determining factors which for the sake of exposition we may divide into two groups. One tendency may be described as Marxist theories of the development of capitalism in backward countries; more precisely, these are extensions and reformulations of the theory of imperialism. Just as the study of capitalist development in the industrial nations produced the theory of colonialism and imperialism, so the study of development in the underdeveloped countries must produce a theory of dependence. The question of imperialism is to be approached from the standpoint of the dependent countries.[2] A second, no less important major source of dependence theory is the ECLA school (United Nations Economic Commission for Latin America) and its attempts, after the failures of its policy in the 1950s, to reorientate development politics.

Although, on account of the scientifico-theoretical viewpoints and specific national experiences of its representatives, the *dependencia* school comprises different tendencies (see § 6), it is possible to discern some important common principles. We shall examine first methodological and then substantial aspects.

3. METHODOLOGY

(*a*) In order to define 'development' or 'underdevelopment' one has to undertake an *inclusive* analysis, which means in particular that social and economic aspects of development have to be investigated uniformly. However, from the start it is necessary to reject 2 scientific and theoretical approaches: a purely sociological explanatory model such as the structural-functionalist paradigm proferred by Merton and Parson, and the purely economic approaches of the ECLA economists of the 1950s, which admittedly criticised conservative economists but did not include societal aspects in their analysis.[3]

(*b*) Any such global analysis of 'development' or 'underdevelopment', which is recommended by Marxists but also by several non-Marxist development theorists,[4] has to be approached *historically*. Then not only do historico-structural conditions come clearly to the fore,[5] but their variability, as it has existed in the past and is fundamentally requisite in the future, becomes obvious.

(*c*) A third common point is that inclusiveness concerns not only the interdisciplinary method but the object under investigation. Precisely because the socio-political and economic structures and processes of a particular country cannot be adequately explained on a national level, the overall system of the capitalist world economy has to be taken into consideration. In terms of model theory, this means that economic external relations (trade, investment, currency, aid) represent extremely important channels of influence and are therefore to be treated as endogenous variables.[6] According to the specific socio-political constellation, they largely determine internal economic structures and processes. A notional restriction to the national economic sphere would be unrealistic both in the case of central and in that of peripheral countries, since it would mean the exclusion of major variables.

4. DEMARCATIONS

Methodologically, then, 2 approaches of development theory are excluded which have moulded the discussion of development for some decades: the stage theory and the dual economy theory.[7]

(*a*) Stage theory maintains that present-day developing countries have to undergo an essentially uniform evolution, to the point of economic and social modernisation, of the kind experienced by the industrial nations in the last century.[8] This kind of theory has to be rejected as anhistorical, since a country's 'development' is decided by specific internal and external historical factors. For a modern developing nation, the close international nexus on the political and economic level which evolved over some centuries, is an essentially different starting-point which cannot be compared with the nineteenth century. Hence merely to adopt development strategies which might have been well-proven in the history of the industrial nations would necessarily be unsuccessful.

(*b*) According to the dual economy theory, 2 wholly separate sectors have to be distinguished in a developing country: the modern sector, which is characterised by the monetarisation of the economy, high rates of growth, (possible) industrialisation, a capitalist mode of production, strong relations with abroad; and the traditional sector, in which a subsistence economy and/or feudalism, natural economy and stagnation predominate, and which offers many obstacles to modernisation and capitalist penetration.[9]

The proponents of the *dependencia* school credit the capitalist economic system with a considerable penetrative power which since the sixteenth century has taken effect in distinct stages, first in trade and later in production—in ever greater areas.[10] The economico- and socio-historical experience of the periphery shows quite clearly that it can be explained only in connection with the system as a whole. It would be far beyond the scope of this article to offer even an historical account of these manifold 'dependences' of the last 4 centuries. We shall therefore restrict our account to the last 3 decades.

5. THE CHARACTERISATION OF 'DEPENDENT ECONOMIES'

In addition to these common methodological features, the *dependencia* school agrees on the characterisation of 'dependent economies' in regard to the following points:[11]

(a) In most developing nations the distribution of incomes is very unequal and in some (though not in all cases) it becomes even worse with economic growth.[12]

(b) The consumption patterns of the élite in the periphery are heavily influenced by preferences that originate in the centre.[13]

(c) The technology used in the industrialisation process is adopted from the centre in a more or less inappropriate form, either by direct investment by multinational companies or by means of licences for local businesses. This technology perpetuates the unequal distribution of incomes and suits the consumer demand of the élite.

(d) There is usually a strong foreign economic presence by reason of the size of the multinationals, foreign aid, foreign loans and trade with the centre. Industrialisation through export promotion or import substitution does not usually reduce reliance on foreign finance and technology but, on the contrary, increases it. There is no local technological progress of any economic significance.[14]

(e) The foreign influence is not restricted to the economic sphere, but takes effect also in the cultural, educational, legal and political spheres. There is no need for any direct form of domination; it is enough to assume that the peripheral areas adopt and extend systems used at the centre, and that the ruling élites ensure an identity of interests with the economic concerns of the rich capitalist nations. This guarantees the existence of a 'symbiotic' relationship between the ruling classes in the centres and the élites, or certain sections of the élites, in the peripheral areas. There is no need to apply a naïve version of a 'conspiracy' theory in this regard. On the contrary, the relationship is open to an extremely complex analysis and can be subject to tensions and change. Essentially, however, it is safe to assume that there are certain internal forces which continually extend the capitalist mode of production and promote long-term integration into the universal capitalist system.

6. EXPLANATIONS

Nevertheless the proponents of the *dependencia* school do not agree on their explanations of the foregoing phenomena. Whereas for Cardoso, Faletto and so on, the *dependencia* approach is only of methodological significance, and has to be filled out with actual investigations which are specific to individual countries, other *dependencia* theoreticians, relying on the Marxist or ECLA interpretations, try to construct a formal theory of underdevelopment.[15]

Both tendencies accord a position of central importance to the problem of growing economic inequality.[16] The first group attributes the responsibility for international and national polarisation to the capitalist system as such and consequently argues for a total delinking strategy (see § 7 (*a*)). The second group, on the other hand, argues for the continuation of the capitalist system with simultaneous promotion of equality: in this case it is a question merely of ascertaining conditions within the developing nations which prevent complete integration into the capitalist system (see § 7 (*b*)).

(*a*) 'Development of underdevelopment'

This is how A. G. Frank, certainly the most provocative representative of the *dependencia* school,[17] describes development in Latin America. Contrary to the viewpoint that development is a preliminary, constantly declining state (as maintained by the stage and dual economy theories), this argument postulates, on the basis of theory and empirically substantiated examples, a relative and at present absolute process of impoverishment of the majority of the population. This kind of thesis deserves to be taken especially seriously and to be tested in detail, if our analyses of the development process are to be governed not by the value judgments of social Darwinism (that is, economic growth at the cost of the weakest), but by values of privileged solidarity with the disadvantaged.[18]

This theory of underdevelopment is comprehensible only if development does not primarily mean growth but greater equality and autonomy. The implication in this connection is, therefore, that the capitalist world economy destroys or prevents development understood thus.[19]

What sort of model accords with this process? Whereas several Latin American authors[20] have investigated the 'mechanisms of underdevelopment' more or less in essay form or in individual articles, Samir Amin (Dakar)[21]—independently of the *dependencia* school, but wholly in the spirit of its Marxist proponents—made an attempt at a systematic explanation, the main lines of which are summarised in what follows:

(i) *Auto-centred or dependent development?*

Samir Amin divides the economic system into 4 sectors: 1. exports, 2. mass consumer goods, 3. luxury consumer goods, and 4. equipment, as in the following diagram, which shows the difference between an auto-centred and a peripheral system:

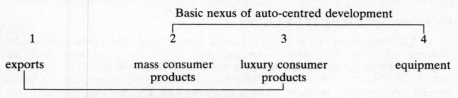

These 4 sectors can be studied both in regard to production and to the proportion of the working population active in these sectors of production.

(ii) *Characterisation of the centre*

Economic development in the industrialised nations is characterised by a preliminary dissolution of the feudal mode of production. The agricultural revolution precedes the industrial revolution. External relations are subordinated to internal development: in other words, the system is auto-centred. The decisive link in the above diagram is that connecting the production of mass consumer goods (sector 2) with the production of equipment (sector 4). The workers' wages occur here not only as costs but simultaneously as income, which gives rise to the major demand for mass consumer products. Auto-centred development understood thus has occurred not only in the western industrialised countries but in the Comecon countries and in China, though in each case in an historically distinct process.

(iii) *Characterisation of the periphery*

For the most part, in the peripheral countries there is no preliminary agricultural revolution. The feudal mode of production largely predominates and agricultural productivity stagnates. External relations are not determined by internal development, but the converse is true: internal development is dependent on external relations (multinationals). The fundamental relation is the connection between export production (sector 1) and luxury consumer production (sector 3). Industrialisation (partly with local capital) is directed towards import substitution: that is, long-term consumer products for the luxury consumer market are now manufactured in the country itself instead of being imported. These goods, with the aid of foreign technology, are produced on a capital-intensive basis and as a result there is a slight favourable effect on the labour market. Foreign capital remains in the country only so long as it can produce higher profits as insurance against higher risks. The lower wages which are necessary for that purpose are guaranteed by the higher unemployment rate. Since the industrial production process is largely restricted to goods for export and luxury consumption, the workers' wages figure for the most part as expenses and scarcely as assets, whereas assets originate elsewhere, namely abroad or in the income of the privileged social classes.

This process perpetuates, on the one hand, in the periphery an extremely unequal (and partly increasingly inequal) distribution of incomes; it leads, on the other hand, to an increasing polarisation to the advantage of the centre. The impoverishment and marginalisation of the masses is the specific condition for the integration of a privileged minority into the world system. It guarantees this minority a growing income which results in the imitation of 'European' consumer patterns. Cultural and economic dependence, and in certain circumstances even political dependence, is then added to the existing technological dependence.

(b) Reformulation of the ECLA analysis

ECLA economists in the 1950s criticised conventional development under the influence of Keynesian ideas.[22] Among other things, in accordance with the Heckscher-Ohlin principle, that theory says that in international trade both countries will obtain advantages from their different local assets (land, labour, capital), if the country exports those products which it produces with a higher asset intensity. An agricultural nation will therefore be at an advantage in producing agricultural goods, whereas an industrial nation should offer industrial products.[23] This theory is restricted to a statistical mode of understanding and is based on unrealistic assumptions. Though additional improvements were made to it, it remained an equilibrium theory, and as such necessarily proved inadequate when—as Keynes supposed—the market economy was not automatically stable, but featured tendencies to disequilibrium on the goods and foreign trade markets. This criticism was supported empirically by the deterioration of terms of trade and the international distribution of labour, which was unfavourable to the developing nations.

To overcome economic stagnation, it was necessary to remove internal and external obstacles to development; this was called 'State intervention' at home, and 'healthy protectionism' as far as other countries were concerned. The increasing economic difficulties[24] and the socialist path chosen by Cuba persuaded several ECLA economists to undertake a more radical critique and reformulation of their analysis. Nevertheless they remained within the capitalist system, but sharply criticised the international and internal tendency to separation and investigated, among other things, the connections between multinational capitalist integration and national disintegration.[25]

Marginality, that is, the internal process of polarisation and stratification, was described as the 'largest and most explosive problem of Latin America', inasmuch as it meant that the majority of the population had no access to an adequate income.[25] The principal criterion for authentic development is therefore no longer growth but a reduction of inequality or marginality. But this goal was blocked by optimally unrestricted integration into the capitalist world economy.

7. DELINKING (DISSOCIATION)

Discussion of economic dependence would be no more than an academic undertaking if it did not involve the conflict about various strategies of development policy. But these strategies depend on what is understood by development. The largely accepted goal of development politics is to engage the greatest possible number of people in productive labour and to satisfy their fundamental needs.[26] But how can this problem be solved operationally?

According to the foregoing analyses regarding the attainment of economic autonomy (which does not mean autarky), a necessary, though not sufficient condition for authentic development is a complete or selective severing of financial relations (not necessary of trade relations) between the developing nations and the centres of capitalism. Complete dissociation means dissociation from international capitalism, and the construction of a socialist society (historical examples are China and Cuba); selective delinking is conceivable under various political régimes.

(a) Complete delinking as a gradual process

The most consistent proponent of such a strategy is certainly Samir Amin,[21] who postulates a transition strategy which is intended to offer a gradual replacement of the model of capitalist, dependent development by a model of national, auto-centred development (see § 6 (a)). Truly autonomous development must necessarily be a form of development which is to the advantage of the masses. Therefore modern technology has to be placed in the service of the direct improvement of the productivity and living condition of the masses. In order to serve the poor agricultural population, industrialisation must be directed from the start to the raising of agricultural productivity. In order to help the urban masses it is just as necessary to surrender the production of luxury goods for the internal and export markets, since both rely on the reproduction of cheap labour forces. A diminution of the unequal division of labour implies, however, a blocking of the exportation of raw materials. The extraordinary resistance which the developed world shows to this is an indication that the centre—in spite of all its fine phrases—is set on exploiting the Third World. If this exploitation were brought to a halt, then the centres would be forced to alter their structures accordingly in order to adapt to a new, less inequitable international division of labour.

The newly ordered form of industry cannot look to the developed countries for ready technological models. Nor can it find them in out-of-date technologies of the centres (intermediate technology). In order to develop an appropriate technology, the autonomy of scientific and technological research in the Third World is necessary. Direct improvement of the living conditions of the masses presumes that distribution of resources will no longer occur in accordance with the law of profitability, but that it will be redetermined outside the laws of the market by means of a direct understanding of the ways in which needs are articulated (dietary, housing, educational and cultural needs).

(b) Selective delinking

The demand for a strategy of this kind is made not only by the political left but sometimes even by the right. Whereas D. Senghaas makes and establishes his plea for dissociation[27] more from a politological standpoint, C. F. Diaz-Alejandro[28] examines selective delinking strategies from an economic angle, some aspects of which we shall now look at.

External economic relations are handled by means of 'international market' for products, technology and capital. In order to design a selective strategy we must therefore ask what is meant by the 'market' and how the contracts made on the market are to be characterised. Adam Smith and other classical authors thought primarily of national markets. These, in order to be effective and work in a decentralised manner, must be located in a framework of legal and ethical norms the realisation of which is to be ensured by the State in cases of necessity. On an international level nowadays it is the industrial nations which essentially decide this 'extra-economic' framework. The markets are unilaterally 'transpoliticised'[29] and characterised by the intolerance of the centre to the selectivity of the periphery. Therefore an international assurance of the selectivity of internationally recognised and applicable rules, of a 'world security system for selectivity',[30] is necessary in order to prevent an abuse of economic power and trade restrictions in particular on the part of the multinationals.

External economic contracts of the developing nations are very often characterised by entire 'packets' of part contracts in trade, and technological and/or capital exchange, which are mostly long term and irreversible. In many cases they have resulted from the pressure put by multinationals on the governments of the northern nations. Accordingly, selective delinking means that these 'packets' are 'untied' and divided into smaller and—if possible—shorter-term arrangements in order to reduce the ties of the southern nations by a greater possibility of choice between many alternatives.

It is obvious that in addition to the political pursuit of a 'world security system for selectivity', in order to effect selective delinking on the international markets and in external negotiations, experts are required who will advise the developing nations in accordance with the criterion of the common good of the nation in question.

8. CONCLUSION

The foregoing should show clearly that as great as possible an integration of the developing nations into the world economic system under existing socio-political power structures is certainly not the strategy that would ensure productive labour and satisfaction of essential needs for the mass of people. Interdependence in international economic relations may be justified as a Utopian goal. If, however, it were actually characteristic of the existing world economic system, the objection that the actual power relationships were being covered up could not be brushed off. Only the rich people of the northern and southern nations would profit from such a situation, not the masses who live in absolute poverty.

Translated by John Cumming

Notes

1. Surveys of the problems of dependence in Latin America: Palma (1978), Puhle (1977); in the Caribbean: Girvan (1973); in Africa: Shaw and Grieve (1977); introduction: Nohlen, Nuscheler (1974) pp. 115-161. Bibliography: Senghaas (1972) pp. 386-399.

2. See Dos Santos (1968). Also Frank (1978). A good survey of economic imperialism is available in M. Barrat-Brown *The Economics of Imperialism* (Harmondsworth 1974). The following are collections of articles on theories of imperialism: R. I. Rhodes, ed. *Imperialism and Underdevelopment: A Reader* (New York, n.d.); R. J. Owen, R. B. Sutcliffe, eds. *Studies in the Theory of Imperialism* (London 1972); H. Radice, ed. *International Firms and Modern Imperialism* (Harmondsworth 1975); Senghaas (1972). A critical survey is available in the article by G. Williams 'Imperialism and Development: A Critique' *World Development* 6 (1978). An important contribution to extending the theory of imperialism is J. Galtung 'A Structural Theory of Imperialism' *Journal of Peace Research* 8 (1971).

3. See Cardoso, Faletto (1969).

4. E.g., H. Bernstein, ed. *Underdevelopment and Development* (Harmondsworth 1973) criticises the inadequacy of the historical approach of the *International Encyclopedia of the Social Sciences*. The historical notion is also absent from J. R. Behrman 'Development Economics', S. Weintraub, ed. *Modern Economic Thought* (Oxford 1977).

5. See Cardoso, Faletto (1969). Important indications in this regard may be found in, e.g., D. C. North 'Economic History', D. L. Sills, ed. *International Encyclopedia of the Social Sciences* V (New York 1972) 468-474, and D. C. North 'Structure and Performance: The Task of Economic History' *Journal of Economic Literature* (September 1978).

6. See Furtado (1971).

7. In addition the *dependencia* school should be distinguished from *laissez-faire* theory (see § 6 (*b*)) and numerous theories which, intentionally or unintentionally, treat as taboo international dependences (e.g., J. Tinbergen *The Design of Development* (1966); T. Haavelmo *A Study in the Theory of Economic Evolution* 1954); or, in part, even G. Myrdal *Asian Drama: An Inquiry into the Poverty of Nations*.

8. The best-known proponent of the stage theory is W. W. Rostow *Stages of Economic Growth* (1960) and W. W. Rostow *The World Economy, History and Prospect* (London 1978).

E

9. The dual economy theory was postulated, among others, by A. Lewis 'Economic Development with Unlimited Supplies of Labour' *Manchester School of Economic and Social Studies* (May 1954). D. W. Jorgenson 'The Development of a Dual Economy' *Economic Journal* (June 1961) and D. W. Jorgenson 'Surplus Agricultural Labour and the Development of a Dual Economy' *Oxford Economic Papers* (November 1967). It was criticised by, among others, Frank (1968) and Martinelli (1970).

10. See, *inter alia*, Amin (1970), Wallerstein (1974), Frank (1978), Cardoso, Faletto (1969).

11. This summary is found in Lall (1975).

12. A survey of recent literature regarding economic underdevelopment and distribution of incomes is found in W. Loehr, J. P. Powelson, eds. *Economic Development, Poverty and Income Distribution* (Boulder 1977) pp. 3-29.

13. See 'Under-development as a process of consumer patterns' in Furtado (1971).

14. See Müller-Plantenberg (1971).

15. Several points for this chapter were taken from Palma (1978). The critical objections to a formal theory of dependence, as Palma and also Lall (1975) formulate it, are indeed worth examining, but appear to be weighted against any attempt to develop a formal theory. They clearly overlook the fact that even concrete case studies imply far-reaching theoretical assumptions.

16. Although classical political economists such as Ricardo considered problems of unjust distribution as the central economic problems, for many decades the question of distribution has either been ignored or treated as taboo by liberal economists. Hence the distribution effects of the market and of growth have been examined, both at a theoretical and at an empirical level, only sporadically and very unsatisfactorily, if at all. This is to be attributed, among other factors (e.g., on account of inadequate statistics), to the fact that the distribution effects of the economic process are of no or only of small interest so long as they are not negative for the dominative countries and interests in practice or in theory.

17. Frank says of himself that he was never desperate enough to claim to be a Marxist, nor did he need to deny being one. Perhaps that was why he was criticised by the most diverse viewpoints. Frank (1977) outlines the controversies about his ideas.

18. This second position is characterised, *inter alia*, by the interest that Frank already showed at an early stage in the problem of the Indians (see Frank 1968).

19. This varying definition of development would seem to be taken too little into account even by the well-intentioned critics of the *dependencia* school, Lall and Palma.

20. The following belong to this division of the *dependencia* school: Frank (1967, 1968), Dos Santos (1968, 1970), Marini (1972), Caputo and Pizarro (1974), Hinkelammert (1971).

21. This very summary acccount was drawn from Amin (1972 and 1977). A more nuanced, extensive analysis on the same theme divided according to areas is to be found in Amin 1(1973).

22. Central articles on the theory of international trade are collected by J. Bhagwati, ed. *International Trade* (Harmondsworth 1969). Prebisch's main ideas are discussed in W. Baer (1961-2) 'The Economics of Prebisch and the ECLA' *Economic Development and Cultural Change* No. 2; E. L. Bacha (1974) 'Un modelo de commercio entre centro y periferia en la tradición de Prebisch' *Trimestre Economico* 303-312; bibliography, L. E. Di Marco, ed. *International Economics and Development* (New York 1972).

23. A fundamental critique of the *laissez-faire* theory is to be found in Diaz-Alejandro (1978).

24. The following deserve mention: the flow of capital assets from Latin America, insufficient increase of actual wages and therefore of buying power, unemployment, increasing direction of industrial production to the profit of the élites without positive effects on other sectors.

25. See Sunkel (1970). There is an excellent analysis of marginality in A. Quijano 'Redefinición de la dependencia y marginalización en America Latina' (Santiago 1970; in photocopy).

26. See the explanation by Cocoyoc, source: United Nations General Assembly, A/C.2/292 I. 11. 1974.

27. Senghaas (1977).

28. Diaz-Alejandro (1978).
29. Cf. Diaz-Alejandro (1978), 127.
30. 'A World Safe for Selectivity' (Diaz-Alejandro).

Select bibliography on the problems of dependence

Amin, S. *L'Accumulation à l'échelle mondiale* (Paris 1970). ET: *Accumulation on a World Scale* (New York 1975).
id. *Le Développement inégal* (Paris 1973). ET: *Unequal Development* (Hassocks, Sussex 1976).
id. 'Sur la théorie de l'accumulation et du développement dans la société mondiale contemporaine' *Tiers Monde* 52 (1972).
id. 'Self-Reliance and the New International Economic Order, *Monthly Review* 3 (1977).
Caputo, O., and Pizarro *Dependencia y Relaciones Internacionales* (Costa Rica 1974).
Cardoso, F. H., and Faletto, E. *Dependencia y Desarollo en América Latina* (Mexico 1969).
Díaz-Alejandro, C. F. 'Delinking North and South: Unshackled or Unhinged?', Fishlow, A., ed. *Rich and Poor Nations in the World Economy* (New York 1978).
Dos Santos, T. *La crisis de la teoría del desarollo y las relaciones de dependencia en América Latina* (Santiago 1978). ET: 'The Crisis of Development Theory and the Problem of Dependence in Latin America', Bernstein H., ed. *Underdevelopment and Development* (Harmondsworth 1973).
id. 'The Structure of Dependence' *American Economic Review* (1970) 231-236.
Frank, A. G. 'Capitalism and Underdevelopment in Latin America' *Historical Studies of Chile and Brazil* (New York 1967).
id. 'Dependence is dead, long live dependence and the class struggle: an answer to critics' *World Development* (1977) 355-370.
id. *Dependent Accumulation and Underdevelopment* (London 1978).
Furtado, C. *External Dependence and Economic Theory* (Elsinore 1971).
Girvan, N. 'The development of dependency economics in the Caribbean and Latin America' *Social and Economic Studies* (1973) 1-33.
Hinkelammert, F. *Dialectica del Desarollo Desigual* (Valparaiso 1971).
Lall, S. 'Is dependence a useful concept in analysing underdevelopment' *World Development* (1975) 799-810.
Marini, R. M. 'Dialectica de la dependencia: la economica exportadora' *Sociedad y Desarollo* (1972) 5-31.
Martinelli, A. *On Theories of Dualism* (Varna 1970).
Müller-Plantenberg, U. 'Technologie et dépendance' *Critique de l'économie politique* (1971) 68-82.
Nohlen, D., and Nuscheler, F. eds. *Handbuch der Dritten Welt* (1974) I.
Palma, G. 'Dependency: A Formal Theory of Underdevelopment or a Methodology for the Analysis of Concrete Situations of Underdevelopment' *World Development* (1978) 881-924.
Puhle, H. J., ed. *Lateinamerika—Historische Realität und Dependencia-Theorien* (Hamburg 1977).
Shaw, T. M., and Grieve, M. 'Dependence or Development: International and internal inequalities in Africa' *Development and Change* (1977) 377-408.
Senghaas, D. ed. *Imperialismus und strukturelle Gewalt. Analysen über abhängige Reproduktion* (Frankfurt a.M. 1972).

id. ed. *Peripherer Kapitalismus. Analysen über Abhängigkeit und Unterentwicklung* (Frankfurt a.M. 1974).

id. Weltwirtschaftsordnung und Entwicklungspolitik. Plädoyer für Diussoziation (Frankfurt a.M. 1977).

id. ed. *Kapitalistische Weltökonomie. Kontroversen über ihren Ursprung und ihre Entwicklungsdynamik* (Frankfurt A.M. 1979).

Sunkel, O. 'Intégration capitaliste transnationale et désintégration nationale en Amérique latine' *Politique Etrangère* (1970) 641-700.

Wallerstein, I. *The Modern World System: Capitalist Agriculture and the Origins of the European World—Economy in the Sixteenth Century* (New York 1974).

Dieter Senghaas

Dissociation as a Development Strategy

1. INTRODUCTION: LAUNCHING ECONOMIES ON A NEW BASIS

FOR DECADES—and in some cases for centuries—Third World countries have been integrated into the still-prevailing international economic order on which there has recently been so much political and scientific discussions. By this integration Third World economies have become growth economies. As a rule, they became vital suppliers of mineral and agrarian raw materials; most recently some of them have succeeded in supplying the world economy with manufactured goods of a low degree of processing.

Since both conventional economic theory in general and conventional development theory in particular have remained growth-oriented, the remarkable achievements of developing countries in satisfying the highly industrialised countries' demand for unprocessed or little-processed raw materials have been considered proof of an adequate development strategy in the short and in the long run. There can be no doubt that average growth-rates of Third World countries during the past 3 decades have been far higher than average growth-rates of the highly industrialised countries during their development since the middle of the eighteenth century. But not only does the economy grow: so does mass misery. This undeniable fact has been well documented by many reports of research institutes and international organisations.

In the debate about the interconnection between high growth-rates and the spread of mass misery, the idea has been recently formulated that the new beginnings of a reasonable development strategy should not be searched for in new modifications of further integration of Third World economies into the international economic order, but rather in a *dissociation* (or *delinking/decoupling*) order (Senghaas 1977). It is assumed that only by counteracting the deleterious reproduction mechanisms of the prevailing international economic order would Third World countries be able to put their economies on a new basis which would enable growth *and* development to be combined within a time-span of one or two generations.

2. THE ASSUMPTIONS OF FRIEDRICH LIST

The idea of dissociation contradicts in many respects the explicit or implicit

57

recommendations of most development strategies. Nevertheless, this idea is not really a new one. One could call it neo-Listian, since its essentials were formulated by the German economist Friedrich List more than 130 years ago. The basic structure of the international economy which Friedrich List clearly analysed is the same today as in his days, although the disparities within the world economy have become far more accentuated in the meantime. List considered himself a proponent of societies like the USA and the continental European States which he considered able to develop themselves like England *if* they would *not*—at least for a while—integrate themselves into a free trade system which at his time was dominated by England as the most productive economy with respect to both agriculture, manufacture and trade.

The development of the productive forces of economies with a lower average productivity than that observable in England seemed possible, once these countries of the second level of the international economic order could protect themselves against the overwhelming competitiveness of more productive economies. Such dissociation was considered a tactical instrument for consolidating the basis of economies with a high development potential, in a short time making them competitive at a later stage. Such a strategy does not preclude the selective and well calculated transfer of commodities, technologies, and skills from economies with higher productivity into economies of relatively low productivity.

List considered the following factors as ingredients of such a basis: the increase of agricultural productivity in order to secure enough food for the local population and to mobilise enough agrarian raw materials for industry; the industrial production of consumer goods available to the mass of the population (*mass* consumer goods in contrast to luxury consumer goods); the development of basic industries and the production of capital goods and of technology. Like the classical British economists of his time, List pleaded for an ever-expanding division of labour while at the same time he strongly emphasised the need for 'confederating' the productive forces—or as we might say today—the interlinkages of manifold economic circuits, including forward and backward linkages. Only after the build-up of such a solid economic basis did List consider the reintegration of such economies into a hierarchically structured international economic order as reasonable and, from the viewpoint of development, feasible.

List's programme of dissociation should not be reduced to a simple economic calculus. As an economist he naturally emphasised the promotion of coherent economic circuits. At the same time, he also emphasises the need for a more effective political steering of one's own development. Such effective steering should lead to the ability to select external dependencies according to one's own advantage. Finally, List was very much concerned about the development of cultural and political identity, which he considered one of the most essential productive forces of a people.

3. DEFORMATIONS IN THIRD WORLD ECONOMIC STRUCTURE

These fundamental ideas do not need re-thinking: they are today as correct as they were in List's days. How correct List was can easily be shown by analysing the basic economic structure of Third World countries, which have been integrated into a—more or less—free trade system. It should be noted that this structure can be observed in cases with a very high *or* a very low population density; in countries with an over-supply or with a lack of natural resources; in economies with a rather high degree of differentiation as well as in economies with monocultural structures.

The basic structure of Third World economies has the following characteristics:

(a) In most cases only export-oriented parts of the agriculture are highly productive (food-stuff, agrarian raw materials); no increase of the productivity of the *entire* agriculture can be observed. Therefore, an essential precondition of a successful development process is lacking. The raw materials production sector is similarly structured. In many cases this production is not interlinked with the local economy; so it must be considered as an exclave-type economy.

(b) Industrial production of mass consumer goods lags behind the import of industrially produced luxury consumer goods—and in some cases behind local production of luxury commodities. This reflects great disparities in income distribution, far more accentuated in contemporary developing countries than in nineteenth-century Europe. If the development process does not lead to the integration of the mass of the people into productive activities—and if there is no rising mass income—then there is no demand for such *mass* consumer goods; the fundamental interlinkages between agriculture and industry do not take place to a sufficient degree; development of the local *internal* market stagnates; and there are no stimuli for profitable investments.

(c) In most Third World economies there is a chronic lack of the production of the means of production (tools, producer goods, technologies). The development of such a sector has been prevented by the integration of these economies into an asymmetrically structured international division of labour: Third World countries supply highly industrialised countries with unprocessed or low processed agricultural goods, raw materials, and with manufactured goods of a low processing degree; whereas the industrialised countries export finished goods, machinery, technology, skills and expertise. In as much as countries of the Third World do not produce the latter goods, they are deprived of vital development impulses, even should the terms of trade between themselves and the industrialised countries be fair (and if there were to be no terms of North-South trade *problématique*). In the very few cases where the build-up of a sector for production of producer goods can be observed, the sector is generally oriented towards already existing growth-poles: it is, therefore, geared to basic goods and producer goods which are prerequisites for the production of *luxury* consumer goods and the corresponding infrastructure.

The production of intermediate goods is also little developed. This constitutes—together with the lack of a production of technology—the basis for the deep technological dependency of Third World countries on highly industrialised countries—a dependency which transfers itself in a deleterious financial dependency (international debt problem).

(d) The growth of the commodities of collective consumption (education, health, etc.) and the development of infrastructure have, in general, not contributed to the homogenisation of Third World countries. Quite to the contrary, they have contributed to deepen the structural heterogeneity of these societies into very few *growth poles* (with a relatively high developed infrastructure) and areas of *hinterland*.

4. THE INVIABILITY OF PERIPHERY ECONOMIES

Friedrich List would have considered such societies and economies as 'crippled' because they lack essential economic sectors and their interlinkages (preconditions for a viable society and economy). The *problématique* of such economies does not consist in a lack of capital accumulation: quite the contrary! In most cases Third World economies are tremendous growth economies; or one should rather say: growth-pole economies in which a remarkable growth is concentrated on specific subsectors—either their output is concentrated on the world market, or their reproduction depends greatly on inputs from the world market.

The chronic deformation of such economies consists in the *non-development of the internal market*. Such economies are internally imbalanced. Their fragility is conditioned by:

> the lack of interlinkage between agriculture and industry and the lack of forward and backward linkage effects;
>
> the lack of coherent and complete economic circuits (demonstrated by imbalanced input-output-matrices);
>
> the propensity of past and present industrialisation processes towards demands of high-income classes whilst the introduction of mass consumer goods had been relatively stagnating, due to stagnant or even negative development of the purchasing power of the mass of the population (peasants, craftsmen and artisans, workers, members of the informal sector);
>
> the narrowness of the internal market, which reflects incomplete and incoherent economic circuits—results of long historical processes with deep structural influence on social structure and patterns of rule.

Such societies and economies are unable to promote certain basic services of viable economies. The mass of the population is not productively integrated into the economy; although more than 50 per cent of the population is active in agriculture, most Third World countries today are unable to feed the mass of their population with locally-produced foodstuff, whilst they often possess flourishing enclaves for the production of agricultural export goods. Hardly anywhere can local production of indigenous technologies be observed. Moreover, there is also a lack of those capacities which would enable these countries to select from foreign technology what seems appropriate and to adapt foreign technologies to their own needs. The demographic development, a reflection of basic social economic deformations, can hardly be managed any more. Against the background of such chronic symptoms, the dialectic of high growth-rates and spreading mass misery becomes understandable; more and more this dialectic translates itself into militarisation processes.

5. THE UNEQUAL INTERNATIONAL DIVISION OF LABOUR

The structures briefly analysed here are the result of the integration of Third World countries into an unequal international division of labour. As yet, the essential different characteristics of metropoles and peripheries have not been overcome; and as yet conventional economic and development theories do not know how to differentiate between equal and unequal international division of labour. All trade is evaluated in terms of comparative costs and advantages, regardless of whether the country already possesses a well-balanced and coherent economy (which becomes increasingly efficient by further exchange processes with other countries), or whether such an economy is extremely imbalanced and becomes less and less viable as the result of its integration into asymmetrically-structured exchange processes within the world economy.

For the political leadership of Third World countries, the contemporary world economic order looks quite attractive—despite all recent criticism. All goods and skills considered necessary for Third World countries can be bought on the world market, if only foreign revenue is available. To buy ready-made commodities is far less expensive than to develop the preconditions for producing such commodities locally. Why re-invent inventions if these inventions are already available and if they can be bought? Why think about appropriate solutions to one's own problems if there are highly specialised institutions in industrialised countries for the solution of such problems?

Such a situation is extremely seductive. The less efficient and less productive economy buys on the world market commodities produced in more efficient and productive economies at a lower price than if these commodities were produced locally. However, there is a problematic trade-off: *fundamental structural deformations*. Although such economies may save certain learning costs, they are finally deprived of their ability to invent, to develop and to produce their own tools, capital goods and technology. This is why Third World countries with a high foreign income have a far more deformed socio-economic structure than do countries with far less international income: the latter cannot afford to buy whatever they want on the world market. The official statistics of Venezuela state that 50 per cent of the population are either unemployed or marginalised; in neighbouring Colombia 'only' one-quarter of the population is assumed to be in a comparable situation. And Nigeria is well on the way to repeating Venezuela's experience.

Recently it has been argued by Jochen Röpke, a national economist from the University of Marburg, that international trade between countries of differing development competence restricts the development potential of backward countries, unless the deleterious influences of the higher competitiveness of the more productive economies are restricted. He further argues that by internationalising the internal market, the creative function of competition within national markets is threatened or blocked.

Why is it necessary, one would have to ask together with Friedrich List (or with Röpke), for a country to produce certain commodities itself although they are available from foreign countries less expensively? Why should one not follow the lure of the world market? Why dissociation for a certain time, if such dissociation may be quite costly? The answer is that only on such a basis is a development process with far-reaching spread-effects possible—a development organically proceeding from simple to more complex structures. If countries shy away from bearing the *learning costs* of their development processes, then there is no prospect for success in overcoming those symptoms which characterise periphery economies.

If the development of national economy is evaluated in terms of criteria relevant for individual business enterprises, it must seem absurd to plead for an autocentric development on the basis of a dissociative development strategy. A national economy, however, is more than the sum of all its constitutive business enterprises, each being oriented towards its own profitability rationale. But still most economists consider national economies and the world economy as the sum of individual enterprises. This is not surprising, since such a view is entirely congenial with metropolitan interests. Should one remind not only the academic community that no single country in the past 200 years (except Switzerland) has developed itself without some kind of protection against other economies of higher productivity and competence?

6. DEVELOPMENT MYTHS AND REALITIES

A new development debate is gradually taking off to demolish the myths of the past 2 decades. The doctrine of free trade belongs to this myth, too. The history of the critical early development phases of England and other contemporary industrialised countries proves just the opposite of what the free trade doctrine has been trying to convey. One has also to say farewell to the myth according to which cheap labour is considered a necessary precondition for development. Quite the contrary seems to be the case. We have to ask why Canada, Australia and New Zealand, although these have been extremely export-oriented and deeply integrated into the world market, did not become monocultures for export-oriented production of grain, timber, furs, etc. In all these cases, the reproduction costs of labour were quite high at a very early stage of the development process. A further myth is the assumption that non-European cultures possess inherent obstacles to development. If this were the case, how is the different development of Japan and China since the middle of the last century to be explained? That small countries are unable to pursue an autonomous development was disproved 150 years ago by Switzerland, with less than 2 million population and without resources. Presently such an assumption is being disproved by small Albania with a bit more than 2 million people.

Conventional development theory states that a 'vicious circle would cause underdevelopment. Nothing is further from the truth than such an assumption. In most cases there is no particular lack of capital in Third World countries, nor is there a lack of growth. But capital accumulation is pursued in tremendously deformed structures which become even more deformed by capital which is not accumulated on the spot but which comes in from outside. *Foreign capital and development aid can help to promote a reasonable development process only when the basis for auto-centred development has already been laid.* In that case obstacles can be overcome more easily with than without international aid. There is, then, very much to be said in favour of international co-operation.

7. THE PLEA FOR DISSOCIATION

The evaluation of a dissociative development strategy depends very much on whether one differentiates between *short run and long run* interests. Such a strategy may seem to contradict also the interests of highly industrialised countries: but only if these interests are calculated in a short run perspective. With long run perspective the picture changes considerably. Imagine for a while that the tremendously large potential internal markets of Third World countries would be developed! Imagine the amount of exchange processes within such a context! Today metropolitan capitalism penetrates Third World countries without being able to really develop their internal markets.

In reality capitalism is acting counter-productively in Third World countries; and there is at present no prospect that a repetition of metropolitan development paths will take place in the future without a break with the capitalist mode of production in Third World countries. Typically, socialism has to be the agent of latecomer economies in developing what Friedrich List expected 150 years ago from the activities of many small-scale industrialists under the protection of a strong nation-State, not to be repeated today under capitalist premises. One need not be an ardent proponent of either capitalism or socialism in order to understand—*sine ira et studio*—the fundamental dilemma in which Third World countries find themselves today.

References

List, Friedrich *Das nationale System der politischen Okonomi* (Tübingen (first publ. 1841) 1959).

Röpke, Jochen 'Der Einfluss des Weltmarktes auf die wirtschaftliche Entwicklung' in H. Giersch *et al. Weltwirtschaftsordnung und Wirtschaftswissenschaft* (Stuttgart/New York 1978) 30-52.

Röpke, Jochen 'Probleme des Neuerungstransfers zwischen Ländern unterschiedlicher Entwicklungsfähigkeit' *Ordo* (1978) 245-278.

Senghaas, Dieter *Weltwirtschsordnung und Entwicklungspolitik. Plädoyer für Dissoziation* 2nd ed. (Frankfurt am Main 1978).

PART III

Attempts at a Christian Response

Hans Schöpfer

The Theological Responsibility for the Human Aspect of Models of Development: A Statement

THE CRITICAL investigation of the humanist bases for models of development is an important contribution Christian theology can make to the discussion of the fundamental issues of the politics of development. Where because of unsatisfactory social conditions human beings live in a manner that is not in keeping with human dignity the first priority has from a Christian point of view to be the struggle for better conditions of life, and this for the reason that the axiom *primum vivere, deinde philosphare* applies to theology too. This plea for a theology that concentrates on the crucial issues while remaining all-embracing gains in topicality if one wants to take seriously the ever more urgent demand for the simultaneous transformation of social structures *and* human beings.

1. NEW PRIORITIES IN THEOLOGICAL COMMITMENT

If one considers the bottlenecks to be encountered in relations between North and South, in which for the most part the western nations still exert the most leverage, the question automatically arises whether Christianity has really done too little for the improvement of social structures, or has it failed in its efforts to make human beings more human (understood as conversion in the integral biblical sense)? The question is justified if one starts from the fact that for centuries Christian images of the world have moulded the West without fully exploiting the chances of social innovation which this provided. It only becomes an idle question if the intention is to use it to shift the blame on to the past or even to be forced to disqualify a particular image of the world. The fact is that even after 2 thousand years' diverse experience the liberating dimensions of Christianity have not been exhausted.

In this there is a sociological datum that ought not to be overlooked. It is that the transformation in practice of a particular way of looking at the world is strongly dependent on a culture's consciousness of value in the wider social sphere. In this there lies a danger of alienation to which Christianity too is exposed. Thus for example the

French Revolution represented an enormous inroad into the 'Christian' understanding of power prevalent at the time. What was unavoidable was that the absolute power exercised by the Fench kings—something many Christians accepted without question— should one day, thanks to an anticlerical opposition, be seen as no longer an absolute. Similarly Christian theology must today look for new ways of co-operation in the social and political field if it does not wish to confine itself to the margin in a world dominated by efforts to balance and reconcile power-relationships that have become polarised. This means that Christian theology must take to heart the criticism that accuses it of a lack of social sensitivity, as for example is directed at it by the liberation theology of Latin America; subjects like justice, solidarity, and commitment on behalf of those at the bottom of the heap must be given greater priority in the schedule of theological work; and the dialogue with theoreticians and futurologists of all shades of opinion from determined non-Christians to theoreticians of growth with their faith in technology.

2. TOWARDS A 'SUBCUTANEOUS' CHRISTIAN COMMITMENT

Understandably the transcendental aspects of Christian existence can only with difficulty be introduced into secularised scientific activity. Nevertheless Christianity contains a plethora of fundamentally humanist basic values which possess explosive revolutionary potential for the development of society (see, for example, the awareness of community to be found in the Acts of the Apostles). Just as the moral basis for slavery was removed by the Christian awareness of the fundamental equality of human beings, something to which not least the French Revolution gave a new impulse, so too Christian *communautés de base* can against a background of extreme poverty demonstrate pioneering forms of living together altruistically, so too political theology can mitigate controversies within the Church by drawing attention to urgent problems affecting mankind as a whole, so too in the face of the threat posed by modern technology in well-off parts of the world Christian love of creation, an ascetic approach to consumption, using leisure for contemplation and biblical optimism must have a more credible effect than ever.

This commitment of convinced Christians on behalf of a world threatened by materialism in both its left-wing and right-wing forms presupposes a new awareness of readiness to be at the service of the world. In all probability social commitment with this kind of motivation has much in common with 'anonymous' or 'subcutaneous' Christianity. It provides the missionary preparation for the actual proclamation of the gospel in a secularised world in which Christians must first prove themselves as human beings. It does not in any case follow the lead of that kind of 'sacramental' Christianity that seeks to overcome unsatisfactory social conditions by purely charitable means or simply shuts its eyes in the face of social imperatives. It also involves a greater degree of risk than confining the practice of one's faith to within the Church, but the original Christian heritage is indisputably reflected if Christians wish to see themselves as the salt of the earth and turn their particular attention to where the need is greatest.

In this way it is not easy for theology to enter the dialogue between North and South. On the one hand theology must regard itself as incompetent in this field. On the other hand in the sphere of what is human everyone, and particularly the Christian, is his own master. Theologians can provide useful additional firepower when it is a question of testing the humanist dimension of models of development. Which theology has to date shown the priorities for Christian commitment in a situation of domination and well-being or dependence and misery so convincingly that these are taken seriously by humanists as well? The following indications of the humanist goals that could be aimed at by new models of development are intended as a pointer in this direction.

3. MODELS OF DEVELOPMENT AND THE NEED FOR A MORE HUMAN DIMENSION

An intensive worldwide concern with problems of development began with the research group headed by Dennis L. Meadows. With the Club of Rome's first report in 1972 on the human predicament[1] full attention was for the first time focused on this scale on the ecological burden. Admittedly, this involved too great reliance on the exponential projection of existing trends. Critics[2] pointed to the significance of mankind's organic growth and to the unforseeable constants this contains. A further dimension, and this time a specifically humanist one, was added by the Cocoyoc statement[3] to the controversy over how different peoples and nations could and should live together. It underlined crucial issues of development, pointed to the lower limits of human needs as well as the upper limits of resources, and criticised excessive confidence in the market economy. The Bariloche model[4] took this diagnosis a stage further by investigating the lower limits set by basic human needs in the form of the minimum needed for a life in conformity with human dignity, the upper limits set by the curbing luxury, and the external limits set by the shortage of raw materials. By describing absolute minima and conditioned maxima it sought not just to avoid purely material bottlenecks but above all to place man, and moreover man as a social animal, in the centre of the picture. The human aspect of social development was thus clearly brought into prominence in contrast to the first of these models of development mentioned. But even this model can still be accused of a certain onesidedness or failure to be completely comprehensive. Insufficient attention was paid to such internal human aspects as thinking in terms of profit, power and consumption, altruism, a basic trust in the essential goodness of human nature and the quality of life; the concept of internal limits could thus naturally be introduced. Here theology is now offered its opportunity.

What it needs to introduce into the discussion, beyond what has already been mentioned, includes the motivation behind a readiness to make sacrifices for social purposes, the bases for international solidarity, the conditions for pluralism and tolerance, and the claims of minorities and of the oppressed. But it also needs to create hope and confidence by demonstrating the human causes of dependence and violence.

So far these dimensions have received their most emphatic expression in the report 'North-South: A Programme for Survival' published by the Brandt Commission in the spring of 1980.[5] In this an international disciplinary team of writers made an independent attempt to work out priorities for a political commitment that would transcend power blocs and vested interests. Among other things it looked to theology for help. Willy Brandt wrote in his introduction: 'The impulses from churches and religious communities as well as from humanism can strengthen world-wide solidarity and thus help resolve North-South problems.'[6] The book offers more than enough material for an intensive effort to grapple theologically with the central problems of the world. A detailed appreciation of the report would go beyond the scope of this statement. But since it ought to mould the political theology of the immediate future attention should be drawn here to some of the basic data it provides. Knowledge of this data is indispensable for shaping the awareness of the rising generation.

Poverty: The World Bank estimates the number of people living in a condition of destitution (and thus in conditions totally out of keeping with human dignity) as 800 million (p. 50).

Starvation: UNICEF estimated that in 1978 alone more than 12 million children under the age of 5 died of hunger (p. 16).

F

Refugees: Of the 250 million people estimated to have fled their countries this century 10 million have still not found a permanent home (p. 112).

Militarism: In 1978 Third World countries' expenditure on arms amounted to $14 thousand million. Since World War II wars in Third World countries fought with 'conventional' weapons have killed more than 10 million people (p. 120).

Energy: One American uses as much commercial energy as 2 Germans or Austrians, 3 Swiss or Japanese, 6 Yugoslavs, 9 Mexicans or Cubans, 16 Chinese, 19 Malaysians, 53 Indians or Indonesians, 109 Sri Lankans, 438 Malians, or 1,072 Nepalese (p. 162).

Multinational corporations: In 1975 direct foreign investment in the developing countries amounted to about $68 thousand million. Seventy per cent of investment in the Third World has been in only 15 countries, with more than 20 per cent in Brazil and Mexico (pp. 187-188).

Who is responsible for all this? There is one thing I am certain of: if it does not make these enormous problems the starting-point for fresh theological reflection and for a more intensive Christian commitment the social theology of the future will not escape the reproach of pharisaism.

Translated by Robert Nowell

Notes

1. Donella H. Meadows, Dennis L. Meadows, Jørgen Randers and William W. Behrens III *The Limits to Growth: a report for the Club of Rome's project on the predicament of mankind* (London 1972).

2. See among others H. S. D. Cole, C. Freeman, M. Jahoda and K. L. R. Pavitt *Thinking about the Future: A Critique of 'The Limits to Growth'* (London 1973).

3. Statement issued in connection with the UNEP/UNCTAD symposium on the use of raw materials, the protection of the environment and development held at Cocoyoc, Mexico, from 8 to 12 October 1974.

4. A. O. Herrera and others *Grenzen des Elends—Das BARILOCHE-Modell: So kann die Menschheit überleben* (Frankfurt-am-Main 1977); (typescript) *Catastrophe o Nueva Sociedad? Modelo Mundial Latinoamericano* (Fundación Bariloche).

5. *North-South: A Programme for Survival*, The Report of the Independent Commission on International Development Issues under the chairmanship of Willy Brandt (London 1980).

6. *North-South*, p. 13. Further references to this report are included in the body of the text.

Marie-Dominique Chenu

The Church's 'Social Doctrine'

1. THE SOCIAL DIMENSION OF CHRISTIANITY

IF CHRISTIANITY, as a religion of salvation, is realised not by a juxtaposition of individual salvations, but by the formation of a people in history, it must have an inherent social dimension, in virtue of which each individual accomplishes his own perfection by and in communion with his fellows. And it is in fact the case that down the ages, in every régime and across the diversity of cultures, Christianity has always involved a collective realisation, the political expression of which was a society called the Church.

There is one thing that is essential and that remains permanent in all this, and that is that this Christian collectivity is meshed into the world in virtue not of power but of the proclamation of the 'good news' to the poor and the little, who, as the first clients of the gospel, are the test of the truth and efficacy of this liberation. It is, therefore, to the extent that it is faithful to this messianism that the Church is at the *service* of the world. These are the axes along which the Christian ethic and the economic realities that are evidently thrown into question by the paradox of the gospel have to be articulated.

2. FROM 'SOCIAL DOCTRINE' TO 'SOCIAL TEACHING' IN ACCORDANCE WITH VATICAN II

The first thing that a historian notes is that this programme, fraught with failures and deformations as it is, does not present itself as something established and organised consciously but as a usually instinctive behaviour in which social practice is where understanding of the economy of the Kingdom of God operates, long before it becomes the subject of theory. It is, of course, possible to pick out down the ages certain clear and vigorous formulations which reaffirm the gospel. But it was not until the end of the nineteenth century that a pope, touched to the quick by the wretchedness of the working people of the industrial civilisation, sought to seize himself consciously, if somewhat belatedly, of the situation and protested against their material and moral distress: in 1891 Leo XIII published the encyclical with the telling title of *Rerum novarum*, 'the world in mutation'. This has justifiably been called the 'charter of work'. This was where talk of the Church's 'social doctrine' began. His 5 successors in office were to make their own contribution to the exploitation of the resources according to the vicissitudes and jolts society and economies underwent. They did not necessarily maintain a completely consistent path and sometimes lapsed into theocratic pietism. The term itself was to become official only in the vocabulary of Pius XII (1939-1958): with him it came to denote not only the content of documents but initiatives, movements, organisations, positions and even (more or less coherent) political options the substantial and even the terminological continuity of which the pontifical documents delighted to emphasise.

Recently, however, not only the imperfection but the ambiguity of the term and the notion have become apparent: Vatican II, in its pastoral constitution on the Church in the world, *Gaudium et spes*, deliberately eliminated the expression and replaced it with formulae that are lexically similar but intentionally different in meaning: the term 'the social teaching of the gospel' speaks of 'teaching' rather than of 'doctrine' and refers directly to the gospel and its inspiration. In this way a dissociation is effected between the general sense of a social content consubstantial with the Christian economy and a particular sense, historically tied to and conditioned by the socio-theological analysis contained in the positions and formulations proclaimed in the texts of the popes from Leo XIII to John XXIII, between 1891-1960.

This discernment which, as we shall see, produced a break in methodology rather than a change of content, was not effected without certain incidents in the process of drafting the texts of the council which are themselves significant. It was not just that the stereotyped phrase was reintroduced subreptitiously and dishonourably after the promulgation by the council (§ 76), but that it was adopted innocently in other decrees of the council, such as that on the apostolate of the laity which was still dominated by the theory of a mandate conferred on layfolk under the influence of the received 'doctrine'. The Latin translation itself lent itself to the confusion between 'teaching' and 'doctrine', which had originally been distinct. On the other hand, in the discussion on the decree on the bishop's pastoral office in the Church an amendment to the effect that a particular ambiguous and disputable expression should be eliminated was proposed and accepted, and it was in fact withdrawn in the final draft.

In order to resolve the subtle but very real ambiguity we must do two things: on the one hand, we have to hold on to the proposition of the episcopal synod of 1971, which sums up the import of the gospel message in a vigorous formula: 'It is quite clear to us that the fight for justice and participation in the transformation of the world are a constitutive dimension of the preaching of the gospel.' On the other hand, we have to recognise the circumstantial and doctrinal relativity of the many positions taken up and directives issued in the wake of the papal encyclicals and not erect these into some systematic, monolithic and universalisable 'doctrine'.

3. THE SIGNIFICANCE OF THE CHANGE IN CONCEPT

The reader may find some difficulty in taking this terminological dispute seriously and sympathetically. The fact is that we are here involved in one of the consequences of the 'Copernican revolution' realised by the council: the world is not made for the Church which supplies the blueprints of its construction and the laws of its transformation in some magisterial and authoritative way, but the Church is made for the world, which is where it exists and which in its self-determination brings to the Church the raw material of its enterprise of divinisation. Just as the incarnate Christ consented to becoming completely human, the Church, the body of Christ, finds its sole existence, *raison d'être*, and power in its involvement with the world. Just as God is from now onwards affected by man's historical condition, the Church can teach only on the basis of the realities of history, according to the rhythms of civilisations and cultures, through a just assessment and respect of the very worldliness of the world. Vatican II had some categoric and moving words to say about this solidarity and responsibility as it was being set up.

Paul VI registers this new doctrinal and pastoral strategy in a modest but astonishingly explicit text, *Octogesimo adveniens*, 1971, § 4:

Faced with such diverse situations, we find it as difficult to make a unique pronouncement as to suggest solutions of universal relevance. This is neither our purpose nor our mission. It is for Christian communities to analyse the particular situation of their country with objectivity, to illuminate it in the light of the unalterable words of the gospel, to draw principles of reflection, norms of judgment and directives of action from the social teaching of the Church as this has been worked out in the course of history and especially in this industrial age, since the historic date of Leo XIII's message on the 'condition of the working people', the anniversary of which it is our joy and our honour to celebrate today. It is for these Christian communities to discern, with the help of the Holy Spirit, on communion with the bishops in charge, in dialogue with fellow Christians and with all men of good will, what are the choices and steps to be taken in order to bring about the social, political and economic transformations that demand to be made in so many cases. In setting about the changes to be made Christians must begin by renewing their confidence in the force and originality of what the gospel brings and expects. The gospel has not become irrelevant because it was proclaimed, written down and lived in a different socio-cultural context. The inspiration it offers, enriched as it is by the living experience of the Christian tradition down the ages, remains perpetually fresh and pertinent to the conversion of men and the progress of life in society, without the need for any reduction of its universal and eternal message by its exploitation for temporal and particular purposes alone.

In other words, 80 years after *Rerum novarum*, Paul VI made a declaration which was overtly in a direct line of social teaching but which in reality reversed the method hitherto used in this teaching: it is no longer a case of 'social doctrine' taught with a view to application to changing situations, but of these situations themselves becoming the theological 'loci' of the discernment to be effected through a reading of the signs of the times. The method is no longer deductive but inductive. During one session of the Commission for Justice and Peace held in Rome (April 1967), Mgr Pavan, who had drafted many encyclicals, underlined the continuity of the teaching of Pius XII, John XXIII and Paul VI: 'Nothing has changed, except that we have moved from theory to practice, that is to say, we no longer make deductions from abstract principles, but we observe reality, for this is where we have discovered the gospel potentially is.'

Nothing has changed, and yet everything has changed. The pluralism that is henceforth to be regarded as the norm is not merely a material consequence of the diverse situations in which Christians find themselves in the world, it is also a matter of principle, stemming from the very nature of the Church which defines itself in terms of its presence in the world and not as an institution endowed with absolute reality. The world is the place where the Christian discerns the appeals of the gospel.

4. CONSEQUENCES

This position and these implications have emerged from experience rather from theory *a priori*. From this it follows that the Christian has not got to look for some 'third way' between the to him 2 equally unacceptable systems of capitalism and socialism, a way proper to him alone, and master-minded on the basis of his moral and social principles as endorsed by the authority of the Church institution. For all that the gospel does indeed make rigorous demands, both of a personal and collective nature, it does not supply some model of society which the faithful are required to promote against others and at their level. The gospel does have a political dimension and it operates in a very real, prophetic way in all situations and all options; but it must not be turned into a socio-political ideology, as has happened, and as some people still want it to happen.

What is fundamentally at stake here is nothing less than our conception of God: we are no longer dealing with a God who has established the constitutive laws of the world from all eternity, who governs by his imperturbable providence, in the face of which the more or less passive docility of human beings guarantees social stability and authority. This 'deism' in which the gospel of Christ is neutralised, was the ideology of the bourgeoisie in the nineteenth century. It did not fail to leave certain traces in the spirituality of the 'social doctrine'. What is, on the contrary, noteworthy is the manner in which the appeal to the message of the gospel in recent texts is given as the reason for the Christian's commitment rather than the requirements of the natural law or some *philosophia perennis* such as Leo XIII advocated with significant consistence.

Christianity betokens an economic order and the kingdom of God comes into being in history, where the contribution which events make is not simply an addition to a vision of man which would exist in its own right, independently of space and time. The Church is led by the new event to a new interpretation of the kerygmatic tradition. We must, therefore, reject an abstract theology which would take into account only the permanent conditions of humanity, whether in regard to its hope or its wretchedness. This sort of theology has in the past served, as it still does, as an ideological sanction for those who hold economic and political power and want to maintain the *status quo*.

Today the development of peoples—*Populorum progressio* (1967) may now already be overtaken but it remains a document of major importance—puts in question the mental structures within which the Church has always expressed its faith. The man whom it saw at the service of a divine order imprinted in nature is now revealed as the architect of his own liberty whose efforts continuously generate the order which enables him to be a person. Turning to the God of the universe and of mankind is simultaneously a process determined by God and an act freely consented to by man. The free acts of man the creator and liberator which constitute history make up the process which, by realising the figure of the world, makes of it a freed world, a saved world. In this way we arrive at a conception of social life which goes beyond the idea of essence in the framework of cosmos and nature and which acknowledges the larger horizon of freedom, time and history. It is, then, no longer that history is a simple modification of some eternal essence but, on the contrary, that nature exists only within the larger framework of history.

5. THE PROPHETIC DISCERNMENT OF THE 'SIGNS OF THE TIMES'

A particular procedure sums up and defines this new strategy: its nerve and thrust is the prophetic discernment of the 'signs of the times', as the evangelical phrase given weight by John XXIII and now part of our currency has it. 'Signs of the times' hits off very well the new effort made by Christians to interpret society and to designate the new awareness of the Church in the unfolding of our contemporary history. Instead of seeking to apply a general doctrine to particular cases, what we must do is to read history as it is, in order to discern its symbolic value in so far the events of this history are where collective experiences crystallise. Reading off the evangelical meaning of events is in no way to abstract them from their earthly reality; it is in themselves, in their own and full density, that they are signs.

At the end of his letter *Octogesimo adveniens* (1971) Paul VI declared, in accents never heard before:

In the face of so many new questions, the Church strives to think out a suitable response of its own to make to men's expectations. Does the fact that the problems seem to be of quite unprecedented amplitude and urgency leave men unequipped to resolve them? It is with all its dynamism that the social teaching of the Church *accompanies* men in their quest. It may not intervene in order to ratify a given structure or to suggest a prefabricated model but it does not for all that restrict itself to recalling certain general principles; it develops by means of a reflection carried through in interaction with the changing situations in the world, under the impulse of the gospel as a source of renewal once its message is accepted in its entirety and according to its demands. It also develops in a manner characteristic of the Church, marked as this is by a disinterested will to service and a concern for the poorest of the poor. And last of all it draws upon a centuries-old hope which enables it, in continuity with its permanent preoccupations, to undertake the *bold and creative innovations which the present situation of the world requires*.

For nearly a century the popes, imbued with their power (*potestas indirecta*!) appealed to the docility of the faithful—to no great effect, on account, no doubt, less of the intertia of Christians than to the ineptness of the method. And now, in the logic of the new strategy, we have an appeal to *creativity* 'accompanied' by the Church. The future is open.

Translated by Iain McGonagle.

John Philip Wogaman

Towards a Method for
Dealing with Economic Problems
as Ethical Problems

1. NEW UNCERTAINTIES IN ECONOMICS AND ETHICS

THE INTERPRETATION of ethical and economic realities has challenged Christian thought from the very beginning, and every age has added its unique deposit to a growing tradition.[1] In our own time, a number of converging facts mark the need for more careful efforts to think economic problems through ethically. The world is more interdependent than ever before, but never has the disparity between rich and poor lands been more starkly evident. The productive capabilities of economic life have exceeded the wildest imaginings of the pioneers of the industrial revolution, but dwindling supplies of non-renewable resources and the hazards of industrial waste and pollution now threaten to limit sharply the future expansion of economic production. Keynesian methods of maintaining economic growth with low rates of inflation and unemployment—though remarkably successful for the period 1940 to 1970—have encountered serious frustrations since 1970. The debate between various forms of capitalism and the socialist alternatives has been joined more sharply than at any time since the period between the World Wars. Economists are much less self-confident about the conceptual independence of their science, and, in particular, many of them are reaching out in new ways to enter into creative dialogue with theologians, ethicists, and other social scientists.

If economics presents us with a confused picture, we should remember that ethics and moral theology are similarly confronted with new uncertainties. At the very moment when people seem more prepared to listen seriously to ethical analysis, the ethicists appear to be more divided and confused about what should be said! Those who would accept the responsibility of entering into the dialogue between economics and ethics must first attend to the questions of method: How do we locate basic ethical norms? And how, once located, can ethical norms be used to analyse economic problems? It is beyond the scope of the present article to offer a systematic treatment of the methodological issues which need to be addressed, but some basic perspectives on method can be presented.[2]

2. THE NATURE OF ECONOMICS AND ETHICS

For present purposes, we can think of economics simply as our understanding of the production and distribution of scarce goods and services. Technologies of production and systems of distribution have varied enormously through the centuries. But all economic activity is concerned with overcoming scarcity and providing people with the things they need or want.

Concerning the nature of ethics, it must be observed that many people have a rather simple notion that this entails only a correct application of authoritative rules or principles to the problems at hand. While this prescriptive mode of ethical thinking has important contributions to make, we must begin to deal with ethics rather at the prior point of determining the nature of the good: What is good, and how may the good be realised in human experience? The definition of the good necessarily entails some unified conception of the highest good or 'centre of value'[3] in relation to which all other things are valued. The determination of the good is the prior question of ethics because without a notion of the good we cannot validate other moral principles or rules. It is because moral principles and rules serve the good that they are binding upon us. Ethical systems vary widely, of course, in their central value commitments; but it is precisely those value commitments that are of greatest importance in the determination of method in ethical analysis.

3. THE LINKAGE BETWEEN ECONOMICS AND ETHICS

The linkage between economics, with its concern for scarce values, and ethics, with its concern for the good, should not be difficult to make. Both seek the attainment of value. But this does not mean that ethics and economics are the same thing. Economics analyses the processes of production and distribution of actual and scarce values—the values that people actually desire—whether or not they *should* desire them. Ethics subjects the values themselves to critical scrutiny in the light of some transcendent source. Ethics, applied to economics, is partly concerned with evaluating the actual goods and services to be produced and distributed. But it is also concerned with exploring the moral values that may be gained or lost through the processes of production and distribution themselves.

Another way of stating the linkage between ethics and economic problems is to observe that even the bare designation of something as a 'problem' presupposes a value frame of reference. There can, at least, be no 'problem' in the absence of purposes which can either be realised or frustrated. The achievement of social justice, as a general purpose, is no 'problem' to self-centred persons who care nothing about the well-being of others and about the quality of life in the community. A 'problem' for such people is defined only by things that threaten their own interests. Even a supposedly technical problem like the overcoming of inflation presupposes the desirability of that goal—and it is well known that some people greatly improve their economic circumstances during inflationary times. For them, inflation may be no problem; *stability* would be the problem! Similarly, racism is no problem to racists, but it is a very serious problem to those suffering from racial oppression. I am not arguing that problems are necessarily defined by social location and self-interest, but that they are defined by values. The task of ethics is to evaluate, to criticise, to elucidate the values at stake in problem situations. There then remain the technical questions or determining how the real good can best be served.

It is also worthy of note that large-scale economic systems and sweeping economic ideologies tend to be directed towards the preservation and enhancement of certain characteristic values. By and large, in fact, economic systems tend to be rather good in supporting the values they are mainly designed to serve. For instance, feudalism has emphasised with some success the values of loyalty and social stability and paternal authority. *Laissez faire* capitalism has centred its attention historically upon freedom and creativity. Keynesian versions of capitalism focus upon productive growth, full employment, and stable currency and, until recently, the record of Keynesianism in achieving these values has been impressive. Socialism has placed greatest emphasis upon equality and social solidarity. Economic conservationism, as it may be called (the 'small is beautiful' ideology) focuses upon achievement of a pollution-free environment and modes of production that are sustainable over the long run. But while each of these tendencies can promise accomplishment in respect to certain values, each also has inadequacies or blind spots respecting other values. So the problem of ethics is to determine which values truly reflect the ultimate good and then to interact with other disciplines in the discovery of the best means of achieving those values.

Our central problem of method, therefore, remains the determination of the nature of the good and the varied forms of realisation of the good in the material world.

4. THE SEARCH FOR THE GOOD ONE CHRISTIAN FAITH

How shall we go about this? In the economic history of the past couple of centuries there has been a strong tendency to identify the good with happiness, and happiness with maximum satisfactions of desire, and desire—ultimately—with pleasure.[4] Thus, the utilitarian principle of the 'greatest good' can be expressed as the greatest pleasure. Pleasure can indeed be treated as the highest good, but not just because it is enjoyed. The reduction of good to pleasure, widespread though it is, does not finally offer us any reason other than the psychological observation that people enjoy pleasure. Who is to say that that ultimately is *good*? Even the less hedonistic ethics of natural law can lack an ultimate basis for identifying the good in so far as it simply identifies the good with observed natural processes. For the observation that something typically occurs cannot convince us that it is good that it occurs.

In face of the problems of identifying the good with purely factual or observable facts or experiences, G. E. Moore warned us that we commit what he called the 'naturalistic fallacy' when we fail to treat the moral good as something other.[5] But if the good is not to be validated by ordinary experience and observation as such, how can we know it?

It seems clear to me that the good is known as such only as it provides an ultimate, transcendent frame of reference for the evaluation of ordinary experience and particular value claims. The most satisfying forms of natural law ethic, and the ones which finally offer most help for economic ethics, are those which consciously seek a metaphysical or ontological point of reference on the basis of which the particular ends and fulfilments of human existence can be located.[6] This cannot be accomplished by simple reasoning from economic data nor even from the observable facts respecting human nature. Rather it must seek to locate the meaning of economic data and human nature in the ultimate nature of reality.

Unfortunately, we cannot claim to *know* the ultimate character of reality, on the basis of which we could determine the good. Even apart from theological doctrines of the fall, we must frankly accept our mental limitations. Knowledge claims are not merely an expression of subjectivism, for they occur out of real encounter with an actual world. But our knowledge of the ultimate meaning of that world depends upon an ability to grasp the infinite with our finite minds. Now, according to St Paul, we only know 'in part'; only later, after we have transcended the bounds of this earthly experience, will we understand fully even as we have been fully understood. The epistle of Hebrews reminds us of the central role of faith in our understanding of the ultimate good, the ultimate frame of reference: 'Now faith is the assurance of things hoped for, the conviction of things not seen. . . . By faith we understand that the world was created by the word of God, so that what is seen was made out of things which do not appear' (Hebrews 11:1, 3). We are always in the position of having to interpret that which is beyond our experience on the basis of that which our limited experience does disclose to us.

For Christians, the decisive revelation of the nature of reality and of the ultimate good is, in some sense, through the person and work of Jesus Christ. In Christ, we understand how the world is reconciled to God with patient, loving intensity. We understand that each life matters to God, and that we exist—whether we know it or not—in the condition of a great human family of sisters and brothers of all lands and races and conditions of existence. We understand that we have the fulfilling opportunity of participating in God's loving and creative purposes. Of course, not all people draw such conclusions from their experience! I believe the central Christian faith to be fully in accord with reason. But I must acknowledge that large numbers of people do not draw this conclusion and instead locate their *summum bonum* in accordance with other experiences and revelations and metaphors. Still, as a Christian, I may rejoice that large numbers of non-Christians share important aspects of the central vision of the good which, as a Christian, I find disclosed in Christ.

Methodologically, I must also acknowledge my dependence upon the witness of the community of faith, the Church. That community of faith exists as a people in history. The traditions of the faithful respecting the character of the good add depth and richness to the perceptions of the contemporary Church, just as the contemporary Church must reflect afresh upon the meaning of the good in new historical circumstances, and just as the contemporary Church must reflect critically upon the errors of the past and learn from them. The community is dependent particularly upon Scripture, which represents the earliest witness to the faith. Methodologically, tradition and Scripture are best appropriated to the tasks of ethics by moving from their profoundest insights into the nature of the good rather than by a simple proof-texting from explicit teachings on particular moral problems—although the latter should obviously be taken seriously as well. Sometimes the deepest theological insights are in some conflict with the more particular teachings, at least so far as the applicability of the latter to contemporary life is concerned.

5. THE ETHICAL SIGNIFICANCE OF ECONOMIC LIFE

What then should be said about the ethical significance of economic life?

Clearly, Christian faith must be affirmative about the material world *per se*, despite the early bouts with world-denying docetism. Christians see this world as having been created by God and therefore as manifesting God's purposes. Perhaps the single most important thing to be said about method here is that we must always evaluate the arrangements of things in this world on the basis of how well or how badly they serve the divine purposes. Do worldly arrangements help or hinder people to believe that God cares about them? Do the actual structures of social existence help or hinder people in experiencing the mutual bonds of loving community? Do people find, in the way life is ordered, a help or a hindrance in finding the liberation of grace? Do social arrangements encourage or discourage sin, self-centredness, alienation? Do natural forces and human institutions provide or deny opportunity for creative participation in God's wider purposes? Do economic realities provide enough security for orderly life planning, or do they contribute instead to chronic insecurity and needless anxiety: do they make it easier or harder for people to encounter the teachings of Jesus about not being anxious over the things of this world as wisdom and not mockery?

Everything about our material and social existence thus needs to be evaluated in terms of its contribution to spiritual ends. And we need to have enough confidence in the deepest truths about our spiritual life to allow it to organise the character of material existence.[7] To the Christian, the spiritual and the material cannot remain in conflict.

Such observations may lead us to several more specific observations about the ethical significance of economic life.

(a) First, economics obviously has to do with basic physical needs: food, clothing, shelter, medical care. Clearly the basic physical needs are requisite to the fulfilment of other moral goods, and thus physical deprivation is a moral problem But on this level alone, hundreds of millions of people are condemned to an existence that is in conflict with God's most basic purposes for human life. The capacity of any economic system or policy to meet the rudimentary needs of all is surely the most elementary criterion of the moral acceptability of that system or policy!

(b) Second, economic arrangements are also important in so far as they provide or fail to provide work opportunity. Work, broadly defined, is necessary to human fulfilment. It is not a curse; indeed, it is the absence of work that is a curse for many people, both the unemployed poor and idle rich. Christian faith sees life in active response, not in passivity. All good work is finally dignified as an offering of grateful service to God. Work is profoundly social in character; it is an outgoing expression toward others, as communication and as service.

(c) Third, economic structures can either aid or hinder a genuine sense of fellow humanity within the human community. This insight may help remind us that 'poverty' refers not only to deprivation of physical necessities, with consequent suffering. It also refers to *relative* want. Even after the basic needs of all people have been provided, so that survival and physical suffering are no longer the issue, we could not ignore the moral effects of great disparities of wealth and income in so far as they create a disposition towards arrogance among the rich and a loss of self-esteem among the poor. Across such barriers it may prove very difficult to maintain the social communion of brothers and sisters in God's human family. The epistle of James expresses both the prophetic heritage of the Old Testament and the ethical implications of the gospel in discussing the deference paid to the rich in church: 'If a man with gold rings and in fine clothing comes into your assembly, and a poor man in shabby clothing also comes in, and you pay attention to the one who wears the fine clothing and say, "Have a seat here, please," while you say to the poor man, "Stand there," or "Sit at my feet," have you not made distinctions among yourselves, and become judges with evil thoughts.' (2:2-4) Sometimes wealthy and poor people have been able to live and work side by side without either being affected morally or spiritually by the contrast. But let us acknowledge that this is a very rare thing in the real world!

(d) Fourth, economics determines important power relationships. Control over modes of production and distribution is often the key to other forms of social control, including politics and government. Ethical assessment of economic problems must therefore also include reference to the ethics of power. I know no way to insure that all will share equally in power; but a strong Christian case can be made for very wide distribution of power and for genuinely democratic accountability of all power.[8] Only thus can we protect the community against the ravages of unconstrained selfishness, and only thus can we avail ourselves of the often-neglected wisdom of those whose powerlessness has made their views easy to disregard. Moreover, human dignity is enhanced and partially fulfilled through responsible exercise of power.

Of course, power questions are central to the contemporary debates between socialism and capitalism: who should control the productive resources of the community and make those economic decisions which shape the common destiny? The debate will continue for some time, since both capitalism and socialism have manifested irresponsible forms of economic power. But there may be important relative differences between typical capitalism and typical socialism at this point. Even apart from these broad ideological and systemic questions, issues of distribution of power and accountability of power are at the heart of the labour-management disputes of western countries and the call for a New International Economic Order between the rich and the poor nations.

(e) Fifth, the definition of private property also entails important ethical questions. Christians must affirm property as a universal right, since property most basically represents protected access to and use of the facilities needed for life in the community. The debates of capitalism v socialism over property refer finally more to the power questions, for it is private ownership of the means of production that is rejected by socialists—not personal property needed for effective living. In any case, the rationale for property rights is not the traditional Lockean one of identifying the right with the act of labour removing 'property' from the state of nature. Rather it is the more radical one of identifying the universal need for property with the wider purpose of God—and asserting the moral responsibility of the community to structure things so that everybody will have sufficient property.

It should be clear from the foregoing that no method can be devised that will yield totally dependable ethical results. Much depends upon actual economic structures and possibilities, including the state of technologies. Christians cannot hope to contribute to the ethical solution of economic problems without acquiring technical competence, any more than economists and policy-makers can expect to accomplish this without giving serious thought to the value considerations which lie beyond economics.

6. DEALING WITH RESIDUAL UNCERTAINTIES

There is, however, a remaining question: How are we to deal with residual uncertainties? When in doubt, how shall we decide and act?

A very helpful method, with much precedent in Christian moral reflection, involves the clarification of those initial presumptions which are most directly in accord with central moral values and according them the benefit of the doubt. Thus, economic practices and policies which appear to be at variance with moral values are forced to bear the burden of proof. That burden can only be borne if it can be demonstrated reasonably that greater loss of the good—as the good is finally disclosed theologically— will occur by maintaining the presumption in force than by abandoning it.

John Rawls' celebrated theory of justice, while it is not based upon theological presuppositions, helps illustrate the point.[9] Rawls argues, in effect, for the *prima facie* moral claim of social equality. Any disinterested observer, who is not affected by a personal stake in the social structure, would have to affirm the desirability of an equal distribution of social benefits and responsibilities. But since the well-being of all may be dependent upon the acceptance of some inequalities of distribution, even the most disadvantaged might rationally prefer the inequalities to greater material deprivation. Nevertheless, the principle remains affirmed that inequalities must be subjected to the test of whether they serve the least privileged members of society—not how well they serve the best off.

The conscious use of presumption may also be the best way to deal with the problem of 'lesser evil' so far as it is to be encountered in economics. To what extent may Christians countenance injustices in economic organisation for the sake of actual solutions that are relatively better?[10] In its general form, this question is not unique either to capitalist or socialist countries, to *status quo* or revolutionary societies. On the one hand we may encounter the problem in the motives of material greed and status competition used to stimulate desired economic behaviour. On the other hand, we may face the claim that autocratic, irresponsible political rule is necessary to guarantee economic stability and productivity under socialism.

In either case, the burden of proof must be against the practices and policies that constrict the moral destiny of people. *Maybe* greed must *to some extent* be mobilised in the form of specific incentives. *Perhaps* political autocracy must be accepted to *a limited degree* and *for a while* to ensure the transition to greater economic justice under some conditions. But we do well to place the burden of proof against even the lesser evils. The Faustian bargains of both the 'left' and the 'right' can so easily lead to greater moral loss than gain. By placing a severe burden of proof against such moral compromise we challenge ourselves and others to devote more creative attention to solutions permitting society to grow morally while developing economically. But still we remain capable of dealing realistically with a world which often forces us to seek the best possible amidst the anguishing moral dilemmas.

Notes

1. See C. J. Cadoux *The Early Church and the World* (Edinburgh 1925); Ernst Troeltsch *Die Soziallehren der christlichen Kirchen und Gruppen* (1911, English 1931); Max Weber *The Protestant Ethic and the Spirit of Capitalism* (New York 1958); Jacob Viner *Religious Thought and Economic Society* (Durham, N.C. 1978) and other standard works.

2. See J. P. Wogaman *Christians and the Great Economic Debate* (London and Philadelphia 1977) for more extended treatment of issues in economic ethics.

3. The relationship between the 'centre of value' and other values has been analysed very suggestively by H. Richard Niebuhr *Radi-Monotheism and Western Culture* (New York 1960).

4. The point almost reaches its *reductio ad absurdum* in the formula by world-renowned economist Paul Samuelson that 'happiness equals material consumption/desire': *Economics* 9th ed. (New York 1973) p. 770. Nineteenth-century utilitarians, particularly John Stuart Mill, are largely responsible for the convergence of the hedonist principle and capitalist economics.

5. G. E. Moore *Principia Ethica* (Cambridge 1903). Moore believed that the good is independent, intuitively grasped quality that is not definable in terms of anything else. My approach to the question is different from his, in so far as I refer the good to metaphysical or theological reference, but I agree with him that it is fallacious, or at least merely redundant, to identify the good with some other quality, such as pleasure.

6. Among Catholic moral theologians, I have found the works of Josef Fuchs and Charles Curran particularly helpful at this point. Protestant writers in the Boston Personalist tradition, such as Edgar S. Brightman, L. Harold DeWolf and Walter G. Muelder, have refined an approach to moral law which may be compared usefully.

7. In his writings on doctrine of creation, Karl Barth's formulations are especially suggestive: 'Creation is the external—and only the external—basis of the covenant. It can be said that it makes it technically possible; that it prepares and establishes the sphere in which the institution and history of the covenant takes place': *Church Dogmatics* III/1 (Edinburgh 1958) p. 97.

8. Note the suggestive formulation on the 'Responsible Society' at the first assembly of the World Council of Churches (Amsterdam 1948), which defined such a society, in part, as one 'where those who hold political authority or economic power are responsible for its exercise to God and the people whose welfare is affected by it.'

9. *A Theory of Justice* (Cambridge, Mass. 1971).

10. In general form, this is the problematic of the 'relative natural law' or of 'secondary natural law'.

John Lucal

The Pragmatism of Church-related Development Agencies

1. INTRODUCTION: THE MEANING OF 'PRAGMATISM'

IN A VOLUME that stresses the ethical and moral dimensions of the economic North-South conflict, the term 'pragmatism' in the title of this article will almost inevitably be understood by most readers in a pejorative sense. Nevertheless, it was chosen explicitly by the committee that planned *Moral Theology* 1980, and this implies some kind of judgment. The context of this judgment is the current of opinion among development specialists and others in the churches that the large Church-related development agencies as a whole have failed to recognise and publicise the importance of the structural obstacles to development and to promote appropriate action at both the national and international levels.

But pragmatism, understood not as a school of philosophy but as a pattern of behaviour that gives priority to experience over fixed principles and to action over reflection, can also be taken in a morally neutral sense: to act pragmatically is not a crime. The following pages, therefore, are not simply a repetition of the indictment of development agencies, but rather an attempt to explain briefly why they behave as pragmatically as they do. They are, after all, merely one set of actors in the development picture, and under the same constraints as their secular counterparts. They are contributing to the total effort of the human family to achieve not only what *seems* to be development, but also a fuller understanding of what authentic development really *is* (the most exciting enterprise today is the 'development' of the theory and praxis of development). No one should claim that Christians are exempt from mistakes, and the need to learn pragmatically from them, in the ongoing search for a more profound understanding of development, based on Christ's 'good news to the poor', the solidarity of all in him, and the coming of his kingdom into this world. These concepts are forcing us to face up to the reality of unjust structures as social sin, and if the large Church-related development agencies have been slow to 'socialise' their notion of development, the same charge could be levelled at moral theology in general, which only recently has moved from an individualistic to a more social frame of reference.

84

2. THE FOCUS OF DEBATE: THE PRINCIPAL CHURCH-RELATED DONOR AGENCIES

The focus of the debate is on the principal Church-related and nationally based donor agencies in the First World, both Protestant and Roman Catholic, which receive large sums of money from highly publicised collections taken up in the local churches, as well as from their own governments, and which then distribute these funds to development projects in the Third World. This distinguishes them from Church bodies at the world level which co-ordinate development activities of donor agencies, from organisms in the churches and councils of churches that are oriented primarily to research and development education, and from Church-related international organisations and activist groups. Out of all these structures, it is the donor agencies which have the most money, power, and influence, both at home and abroad.

Yet even a narrow focus on the large donor agencies is still too wide to permit, in a short article, anything more than a series of broad generalisations about them as a class, prescinding from many important differences. It would be impossible in the space allowed merely to describe each agency briefly, to say nothing of a balanced analysis of how each has coped with the changing understanding of development. Nevertheless, there is much that can be said of them as a collective factor in the overall development effort of the churches.

The donor agencies may be classified as Church-related, nationally based, transnational actors in development, influencing the economic, social and spiritual orders. In terms of world politics, they are 'international social forces' of importance, and play a significant role in the North-South dialogue, even though they are not directly involved in the negotiations. The agencies transfer considerable economic resources and technology from North to South, and although it would be naïve to rank them as major economic forces in comparison with transnational corporations and governmental agencies, they are able to influence to some extent the policies of the latter and of their secular counterparts among the voluntary agencies. Perhaps even more important, they are in a position to shape public opinion through the publicity given to their fund-raising appeals in the North and thus put pressure on governments to improve their aid programmes, while in the South their projects inevitably influence, for better or worse, the awareness and expectations of the poor. Potentially the donor agencies could perform the most important function of all: the promotion of a sense of global solidarity that would make feasible the slowing of growth and development of new life-styles in the rich countries—and among rich élites in the poor countries. Without this transformation of values, essential structural changes in society will be extremely difficult to achieve without a resort to violence.

3. CRITICISM OF THE DONOR AGENCIES

As a class, the donor agencies have been criticised for some five years or more for their failure to keep pace with the evolving theory and praxis of development advocated by many experts inside and outside of the churches. More specifically, the indictment includes several charges. The first is that although the agencies have moved from their earlier concept of aid as caritative or emergency relief (for which they were criticised in the 1960s) to one of aid as transfer of resources for self-help, they have failed to make the further transition of seeing aid as necessarily including the promotion of structural changes in society to remove obstacles to development. Secondly, and as a consequence, they have located the problem of development exclusively in the Third World and its solution largely in the First, a dualism which makes underdevelopment purely an endogenous phenomenon caused by factors in the South (a 'blame the victim' psychology), which have prevented it from 'catching' up'. Thirdly, in taking this position the agencies have ignored the question of justice, for they say nothing of the gross injustices perpetrated on the South by the North, both in the colonial period and the present period of neo-colonialism. Lastly, the donor agencies have not faithfully reflected the latest social teaching of the churches, but have instead followed pragmatically the policies of governments in the North which give them money to promote a development without justice in their fund-raising appeals, thus blunting the prophetic witness of the Church and misleading its people by not telling them the uncomfortable truth, lest they not contribute.

These are just some of the main points of the indictment. It has been presented in greater detail, with evidence, in the excellent work by Jørgen Lissner, *The Politics of Altruism*, A Study of the Political Behaviour of Voluntary Development Agencies (Geneva, Switzerland: Lutheran World Federation 1977), to which the author of this article is greatly indebted, and to which its readers who desire more information are referred. However, since most of Lissner's source material dates from 1975 and before, the question to be discussed is not only the original indictment, but also to what degree the donor agencies have, in the last five years, revised their own analysis of the development question, their screening of development projects, and especially their programmes of development education in the churches. Does the indictment still hold?

4. PATTERNS OF DEVELOPMENT IN RELATION TO THE ROLE OF THE AGENCIES

As noted above, the whole concept of development and of the role of Church-related donor agencies has been evolving in the last two decades. Charges levelled against the agencies must therefore be seen against the background of this process, since the criticism is basically that they have been guilty of a time-lag which is longer than reasonable, and which they in turn have communicated through their fund-raising techniques to the whole People of God. A certain time-lag between advanced research and popular acceptance of its conclusions is normal and unavoidable; the question here is the difficult one of whether the donor agencies have in this case consciously inhibited a process with which they themselves previously co-operated. A rapid survey of the origins and evolution of development assistance by the churches should thus help to clarify the debate.

Lissner reproduces in his book a very interesting chart showing different responses to the problem of world hunger by Christians of the West. Taken from the magazine of the World Council of Churches, *One World* (No. 12, December 1975, p. 21), this chart is still a valid schema of Christian responses not just to world hunger, but to the whole problem of development as well (the adaptation can easily be made by the reader, who is advised to consult the chart at this point and as the article continues). There is a striking correspondence between the four kinds of responses described by the chart and the evolution of development assistance, a process in which the Church-related donor agencies have taken part along with everyone else, with a corresponding evolution in their programme of development education.

(a) Inter-Church Aid

Since the outburst of missionary activity in the last century, the churches of the North have regularly given material assistance to their daughter churches in the South, through what is now called *inter-church aid*, i.e., aid to churches which are not yet self-supporting. This kind of aid has produced problems of its own—such as the creation of patterns of dependence and subjection, with a consequent call for a 'moratorium'—

Different responses to 'world hunger' by Christians of the West

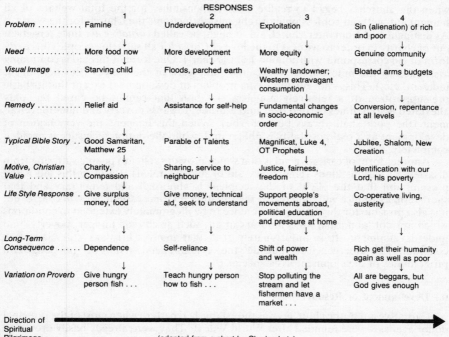

	RESPONSES			
	1	2	3	4
Problem	Famine	Underdevelopment	Exploitation	Sin (alienation) of rich and poor
Need	More food now	More development	More equity	Genuine community
Visual Image	Starving child	Floods, parched earth	Wealthy landowner; Western extravagant consumption	Bloated arms budgets
Remedy	Relief aid	Assistance for self-help	Fundamental changes in socio-economic order	Conversion, repentance at all levels
Typical Bible Story ..	Good Samaritan, Matthew 25	Parable of Talents	Magnificat, Luke 4, OT Prophets	Jubilee, Shalom, New Creation
Motive, Christian Value	Charity, Compassion	Sharing, service to neighbour	Justice, fairness, freedom	Identification with our Lord, his poverty
Life Style Response .	Give surplus money, food	Give money, technical aid, seek to understand	Support people's movements abroad, political education and pressure at home	Co-operative living, austerity
Long-Term Consequence	Dependence	Self-reliance	Shift of power and wealth	Rich get their humanity again as well as poor
Variation on Proverb	Give hungry person fish ...	Teach hungry person how to fish ...	Stop polluting the stream and let fishermen have a market ...	All are beggars, but God gives enough

Direction of Spiritual Pilgrimage ➤

(adapted from a chart by Charles Lutz)

'Development Education': meanings for Christians in the West

Subject	Need for relief overseas	Development projects overseas	Injustice/oppression/ exploitation both at home and overseas	Need for total liberation of all
Method	I tell or show you (because you do not know)		You and I together search for knowledge (dialogue)	
Aim	Sympathy, giving	Sympathy, giving, understanding	Awakening, commitment to struggle	Integration of faith and politics, action and contemplation, conflict and reconciliation

but it is not directed primarily to socio-economic welfare, and so does not appear on the chart. It is to be noted, however, that the Church-related donor agencies are valued by governments because they used Church networks in the distribution of aid.

(b) 'Caritative' Aid

A second type of material assistance by the churches emerged from inter-church aid when the churches began to realise their responsibility for the total welfare of all humankind, without confessional or religious distinction ('the Church for the world'). As distinguished from inter-church aid, it might be called *caritative aid* since it is given out of charity in order to witness to the love of Christ for all suffering people (this early form of aid corresponds with column 1 of the chart). One form of this aid is continuing assistance to the unfortunate who cannot take care of themselves (the sick, aged, indigent, etc.). This is not related to the problem of development except that its basic pre-supposition of a relatively hopeless situation that cannot be cured but only alleviated is sometimes carried over into attitudes towards poverty and underdevelopment (the poor shall always be with you). When this happens the very notion of development as a real possibility is obliterated, while the notion of justice is avoided completely.

Another form of caritative aid is that which provides relief to people suffering from disasters of various kinds (emergency aid or disaster relief). Basic to this aid is the presumption that the plight of the recipient is abnormal and temporary and that short-term assistance will soon rectify the situation. In some cases it does, of course, but it is also possible for this frame of reference to be illegitimately extended to conditions which are not 'abnormal' or temporary at all, such as chronic hunger, poverty, and underdevelopment. It is unfortunately true that many Christians still view such conditions as emergencies, 'outside the system', and requiring no long-term programmes of development assistance.

(c) Development or Resource Aid

Caritative aid by the churches was the established pattern when most of the principal donor agencies were founded after World War II. They were already busily providing such aid when the concept of international development gradually began to take shape in the 1950s and led to the proclamation by the United Nations of the First Development Decade in 1960. For most agencies and for many Christians it was a difficult transition from caritative to *development aid* (column 2 on the chart)—from food distribution to development projects, from dependence to self-help and self-reliance, from simply giving a man a fish to teaching him how to fish. And, of course, the older forms of aid had to be continued. The agencies were criticised for their slowness, but they did make this transition successfully within the First Development Decade, and participated eagerly in the attack on world poverty and underdevelopment through the transfer of resources (capital, technology, education, etc.) from North to South. Today this first form of development aid is often called *resource aid* (at that time no other form was thought to exist). Resources are transferred within existing political, social and economic structures—all of which are assumed to be satisfactory, or at least tolerable contexts in which development can take place.

Resource aid is still development aid in its classical sense, and still prevails in the North, despite the evident failure of 2 Development Decades. Characteristic of resource aid, as it has been practised in the past 2 decades, are an emphasis on economic as opposed to social and political development, overly rapid industrialisation and neglect of the environment, the transfer of advanced technology which is inappropriate to existing cultural and social patterns in developing countries, foreign investment and control by transnational corporations, the creation of élites in the South and a 'trickle down' theory of wealth, low priority to satisfying the basic needs of the poor, and lack of concern for justice and social change. It must be said, however, that resource aid given by the Church-related donor agencies has, by and large, not directly contributed to these abuses, because of its smaller scale and closeness to the people. But the agencies have not publicly pointed out and condemned such injustices, which are part of a system in which they participate.

In theory, the transfer of resources from North to South need not be accompanied by these evils, but in practice it has. This is undoubtedly due to the main theoretical deficiency of the concept of resource aid, namely, its exclusion of the structural factor from its analysis of development. For it is unjust structures which are the principal obstacle to the success of resource aid, whether by perverting the transfer of resources from the start, or by negating the benefits which a proper transfer of resources could bring. The result is that the rich still get richer while the poor get poorer.

(d) Structure Aid

The failure of development assistance based purely on the concept of resource aid was obvious to many by the opening of the Second Development Decade in 1970. Something more was needed, and there followed the call for a New International Economic Order, a structural reform of the global economic system, plus other changes, such as the regulation of transnational corporations, promotion of the agricultural sector and appropriate technology, emphasis on the basic needs of the poor, land reform and people's participation in the South, and less extravagant lifestyles in the North. This contemporary campaign is well known and need not be further described here. It is, in short, a call for structural changes in global and national institutions, based on justice. For this reason, this concept of development aid has been called *structural aid*, although there would be advantages in using the simple term *justice*. At any rate, it is clearly outlined in the set of perceptions and responses listed in column 3 of the chart. Rightly feared by many to be political—because structural change requires political action—and radical—because this change must be profound—this view is nevertheless gaining ground rapidly, particularly among those Christians actively concerned about justice and the future of mankind. The challenge to the donor agencies to adopt this position has come from this prophetic sector within the Church.

5. THE DIFFICULTIES OF THE TRANSITION FROM RESOURCE AID TO STRUCTURAL AID

It seems a fair judgment to say that the donor agencies as a class have, in the last 5 years, been struggling with difficulty to make the transition from resource aid to structural aid (from column 2 to column 3 on the chart). There has been forward movement, yet it has been painfully slow, slower in fact than the transition from caritative to resource aid (column 1 to column 2) in the 1960s. This is most evident in the agencies' programmes of development education, which still use traditional appeals, but less so in their screening of projects, where some significant progress has been made. The forward movement has been greatest in the agencies' own analysis of the development problematic: their own experts understand quite well the need for structural aid. This is not surprising, for advanced social thinking in the churches had advocated it for half a decade at least, and has even, in a growing number of cases, moved beyond to a concept of development in solidarity (column 4 on the chart). Thus the question arises: what factors are responsible for this considerable delay in the practical implementation of structural aid by the donor agencies?

The answer has, of course, already been suggested in certain quarters: the agencies are guilty of pragmatism because they put their own self-interest—good relations with their sources of funds (local congregations and national governments)—ahead of truth and justice. Phrased in this way, however, the answer is basically false. The agencies, like all human organisations, are trying to preserve both their principles *and* their legitimate self-interest, sometimes using pragmatism to make this reconciliation, which in their particular situation they find very difficult. The answer is also simplistic, for it overlooks the limitations of the role which the agencies must play as extensions of the churches in the task of world development, as well as the extreme seriousness of the step they are being urged to take. Yet the answer does contain elements of truth which call for an explanation, at least, although not an absolute verdict. Here again, reference must be made to the study by Lissner, and to his abundant sources, where the issues are treated in much more detail than is possible here.

It is clear that the donor agencies would defeat their own purpose if they alienated their primary constituency, the local congregations whom they serve by sensitising them to human needs and channelling their contributions to meet those needs. They must be ahead of the people, but not too far: as diaconal bodies which raise and distribute funds they do not have the fearless freedom enjoyed by prophetic elements in the Church. True, they have a teaching function in their development education programmes, but its success also depends upon the confidence of the local congregation, which must be brought gradually to enlarge its horizons; no other didactic would be successful. This is not pragmatism, but sound pedagogy. The question of how this division of labour in the donor agencies might best be structured is a complicated one, and has been discussed at length elsewhere (*Lissner*, pp. 279-298). The point here is that the donor agencies are constrained by the level of awareness in their primary constituency, the People of God. And the fact is that in their current understanding of the development problematic, the People of God today have not, as a whole, advanced beyond the concept of resource aid.

And so the question is a larger one: why has the awareness of Christians as a whole not made the transition from resource to structural aid? The accusers of the donor agencies blame them, but this is to argue in a vicious circle. There are other elements in the Church which are more responsible than the donor agencies for the development of the moral conscience of the faithful: Church leaders, teachers, preachers, prophets, lay organisations, and especially, in this case, those organs of the churches which specialise in development education itself. Unless it is argued that the donor agencies have been working *against* these other elements in the churches, a conspiracy theory which is plainly untenable, then responsibility for the slow pace of development education must be shared by them as well, and not attributed solely to the donor agencies.

It is true, of course, that all of these elements could have worked harder at their task of development education—that is merely to make a statement about human nature. But in fact they deserve high praise for their efforts, given their often limited resources and the magnitude of their task, which has been underestimated in the present debate. It is not only that the churches should find the ways and means to work harder; it is rather that their task of raising awareness about development has itself become harder: the transition from caritative to resource aid in the 1960s was a relatively simple one compared to the much more difficult transition from resource to structural aid that is the challenge of the 1980s.

This challenge needs to be examined more carefully than it has: one cannot simply assume that all of the steps in the process of development education will be equally easy or difficult. In this case the next step is very difficult, for 2 principal reasons. First, the notion of structural aid contains a strong emphasis on justice, which for some reason is more difficult for Christians to accept in their social morality than the more ego-satisfying motive of charity. Second, structural aid, by requiring profound social change, in turn requires political action to bring about this change: it necessarily *politicises* the theory and praxis of development aid. And since it is impossible to have political action without some kind of ideology to guide it, structural aid in concrete situations must necessarily be linked to a specific ideological context. But the churches of the North, for historical reasons of considerable merit, do not wish to engage in politics or to be identified with particular ideologies. Perhaps they will have to be, but this is a problem too vast to discuss here, and it is certainly not the responsibility of the donor agencies to solve it. The best they can do is to deal with individual situations as best they can, maximising beneficial social change and minimising their own political and ideological involvement. But this is precisely to act *pragmatically*.

There are other charges against the donor agencies which can be dealt with only briefly. It is true that by accepting large sums of money from governments they have at times compromised themselves, by becoming instruments of national foreign policy, wittingly or unwittingly, or by conforming to secular standards of development in their projects to the neglect of Christian values. Here the temptation has been great, for without these funds they would be able to do far less in the relief of suffering. But that is not a valid defence, for governmental or secular voluntary agencies could perform the same functions.

The donor agencies have also succumbed to other bureaucratic temptations, such as empire-building and competition with other agencies for publicity and praise. They have failed for the most part to play a strong advocacy role with governments, in order to correct evils in national development policies. And they have kept a discreet silence about the immoral conduct of certain transnational corporations, although even Lissner holds that this has been done more out of a fear of becoming involved in controversy than from any less worthy motive (*Lissner*, pp. 121-124). They have practised paternalism in their relations with partners in developing countries, and cultural imperialism in their screening of projects, imposing upon the South the development models of the North. No defence is offered here for these failures, except to note that they are failures primarily of weakness (pragmatism in the bad sense), not bad will; that there are few secular agencies that have not been guilty of the same conduct; and that the donor agencies themselves have frequently admitted their mistakes and taken measures to correct them. On the positive side, of course, the good which they have accomplished far outweighs these deficiencies.

The donor agencies are part of the Church, not much better or worse than the People of God whom they serve in serving the world. And so if they are to take a bolder, more Christian approach to development aid, then they need the support of the whole Church, and the churches in the Church. For this, the Church itself must change, must develop. The challenge of justice through structural aid requires a total effort: better communication of the social message of the Church to the people, closer linkages between prophetic elements and official structures, more effective co-ordination of the donor agencies, and a stronger commitment by everyone to social change. At stake is the whole question of the mission of the Church to the world.

6. TOWARDS SOLIDARITY AS A NEW BASIS FOR MUTUAL DEVELOPMENT

The future does not look bright. Humanity is in the midst of conflict, often violent, and a structural arms race which threatens it with extinction. The oppression of the poor increases and the insensitivity of the North towards the South continues as the global economic situation worsens. It is dubious if structural aid can succeed in this atmosphere of selfishness, fear and hatred, where the call for justice stands little chance of being heard. The only solution seems to lie in a rapid and simultaneous diffusion of the concept of solidarity as a basis for mutual and fraternal development aid (column 4 on the chart). This concept, which aims at reaching justice through authentic love, has already taken hold in certain sectors of the Church. It would be easier for the donor agencies to promote structural aid in a climate of solidarity than in a climate of hatred. Whether they will adopt this strategy, or whether it will succeed, remains to be seen. It seems safe to predict, however, that whatever happens in the near future, the Church-related donor agencies will continue, of necessity, to proceed with pragmatism. The way is too uncertain to do otherwise.

Gustavo Gutiérrez

The Violence of a System

THE POVERTY in which two-thirds of the world's population live is the widest and deepest challenge facing the Christian conscience today.[1] It is not just a social and economic fact, it is a question of justice and love, and therefore an ethical demand. This is not to put the matter on the serene level of principles, nor to seek a facile comparison between this problem and other major human concerns, nor to suggest a call to merely personal responses. It is to suggest, on the contrary, the radical nature of what is at stake: the very meaning of human life and the collective course of humanity. A more rational economic theory or a juster social structure would be no more than the expression—which is of course also needed—of a human approach different in quality; the expression, but also, through a circular relationship, the necessary condition for bringing this different human quality into being. To set this in a properly theological focus: the gratuitous gift of sonship permanently offered by the Father is accepted only in the struggle to create a genuine human brotherhood in history. The kingdom, precisely because it is promise and grace, is the reason for, and the motive of, justice and freedom, peace and love.

All these big words—justice, freedom, peace and love—are continually manipulated to serve the interests of those who deny them—even to themselves—by building a social order on exploitation and plunder of the majority of the people. But this does not, surprisingly perhaps, prevent them from remaining the tersest expression of the deepest aspirations of humanity, the basic impulses to generosity and the driving forces of historical movements. The poor nations are making it increasingly clear that these aspirations point out and enrich the ways that lead to defence of a basic requirement: *the right to life*. This is in effect the basic level on which discussion of economic and social matters, the struggle for liberation, the building of a just society and the evangelical witness of the love of God in the countries of the Third World must take place. It is a simple basic level, but the level that affects the bulk of the population in their daily lives. A document signed by more than a thousand priests and religious working in my country, Peru, contains the following by way of illustration: 'At the weekly meeting for reflection in a suburban parish, an old lady said: "As I have lived a long time, I am getting ready to die; we old people are closer to death". A young man immediately replied: "No, grandma; that was true once, but now it's the children who are closer to death." '[2] Once you grasp this, you have reached the basic level.

Defence of life has always been one of the lynchpins of ethical behaviour in the Christian tradition. Though not devoid of certain ambiguities,[3] it remains a basic

93

requirement. But the situation of the poor masses of the world, dispossessed, marginalised and hungry, is a more radical and coherent challenge. Furthermore, recognition of this is a condition for the credibility of the Church in its fight for the right of the unborn to life, in its rejection of war as a solution to human conflict and of other assaults on human life.

This basic level of life and death explains the sense the poor and oppressed give to their struggle for a full liberation embracing all dimensions of human existence. In the dialectic between the life of faith and material life (the plans on which the poor are dispossessed and their most basic rights violated), denunciation of the sin of an oppressive system and the ethical example of the disciples of Christ come between faith in the resurrection and the death of the body.

1. A SITUATION OF SIN

The poor and oppressed majorities of the Third World countries live in a situation in which their most basic human rights are constantly violated. This is what in Latin America, a continent in which the majority is poor and Christian, has been categorised as a state of 'institutionalised violence'.[4] It is violence because it effectively deals in negation of and contempt for human life. It is institutionalised because it is not something fleeting or occasional, but a social system built on, institutionalised in, the death of the poor for the profit of the few.

The expression may seem strident, even exaggerated, to those for whom these deaths are a matter of statistics and not of everyday experience. But the daily occurrence has to be seen in its dimension of challenge to every human being and therefore to every Christian.[5]

This reality of death, of 'institutionalised injustice' and 'permanent violation of human dignity', as the Puebla Conference expressed it, is not just a description of the hunger, sickness, illiteracy and lack of freedom of the poor of Latin America. This is the state of *oppression* in which they live, brought about by the *repression* practised on them by the defenders of the prevailing social order in the face of any attempt to question their privileges.[6] This makes the situation even more acute and conflictive, but also shows that merely describing the reality does not enable one to grasp the whole of it. We need to go behind it to its causes in order to explain the severity of the repression; failure to analyse them rules out the possibility of defining the ethical need to change an inhuman state of affairs. This is why both Medellín and Puebla denounce the situation of poverty as the result of the prevailing social order, of a socio-economic structure; and as the result of a 'structural conflict' in which the riches of the few are won at the expense of the many.[7] The causes of the conflict are more sophisticated: they exist on the plane of international capitalism, external dependence, multinational corporations, etc.

All this categorises what both Medellín and Puebla call a 'situation of sin', or 'social sin'. This is a theological judgment on a social reality, not socio-economic analysis, which cannot state that a situation exists where there has been a break in the friendship between God and mankind, that is, sin; such a judgment has to come from another standpoint. If the poverty produced by injustice enshrined in a social system is a sin, this is because it works against the kingdom proclaimed by Jesus: has done and does, here and now. Accepting the kingdom in history leads to the requirement of building a just and human society; doing otherwise means accepting and participating in a situation of sin.

If the standpoint adopted by the theology of liberation on this point has one constant feature, it is its rejection of the ingenuous optimism of the theologies of progress, which fail to give sin its due place in the course of history. Not sin as a private, intimate occurrence, needing only 'spiritual' redemption, without questioning the social order we live in; rather, we are dealing with sin as a social, historical event, a lack of brotherhood and a break with God, and a personal, inner cutting-off because of this. Sin occurs in oppressive structures, in the domination and plunder of nations, races and social classes; what is opposed to the kingdom of love and life is thus seen to be the ultimate root of a situation of injustice and exploitation.

These basic statements do not seek to pass over the structural causes of poverty, which have been touched on earlier. They are intended to record the judgment that this situation deserves when confronted with the hope of the kingdom, and so to embrace the human reality in all its complexity and depth. However traditional this may appear, an ethic based on theological reflection on liberation cannot ignore the role that sin, negation of the God of love in the rejection of one's brother, plays in its analysis and its proposals. The social system that sows death appears in its full cruelty and perversity when seen in the light of the kingdom of life. This perception has become acute in recent years, but it has historical antecedents.

2. GOLD AND DEATH

A vitally important event in the history of humanity took place in the fifteenth and sixteenth centuries: the meeting between peoples whose development had taken place in isolation from each other. This gave rise—thanks to Francisco de Vitoria and others—to new views of the rights of nations and the concept of international law. This was an attempt to set relations between different nations on an ethical footing. These first steps are an interesting subject for reflection, since what happened in America—the Indies as it then was—is often referred to as the starting-point for this reflection on questions of international morality. But the truth is that the richest and most evangelical part of the 'Indian' experience did not find its way into the system.

The inhabitants of the so-called Indies had been suffering occupation, maltreatment, exploitation and death at the hands of those who saw themselves, from their own point of view, that of 'western Christian civilisation', as the discoverers of those lands, for 19 years, when their sufferings—being treated like 'animals without rights' by those whose only aim was to 'become rich through the blood of these wretches'—led a group of Spanish religious to 'join law with fact'. That is, led them to unite reflection to their knowledge of the situation and to confront this oppression with 'the law of Christ'.[8]

In sermons which have become famous, they denounced the oppression to which the Indians were being subjected. Their ideas, as always in such cases, were considered new and dangerous, besides being contrary—as both the King of Spain and their metropolitan religious superior stated—to the objective of salvation in Jesus Christ. What is interesting now is not so much the history of the debate, but the reasons given by these friars for their defence of the Indians.

In letters back to Spain, these Dominican friars attacked the social and economic order in course of implantation, which they declared contrary to divine, natural and human laws. They thought this could be demonstrated in many ways, but rather than subtle reasoning, one massive fact struck them as being the best proof: 'all these Indians have been and are being destroyed body and soul, and in their posterity . . . in such manner that they can neither be Christians nor live'. This was the starting-point of an argument in favour of the natives that was to be taken up later by Bartolomé de las Casas, and has since been common to most who have taken up the cause of the oppressed: the fact of unjust death inflicted on the poor.

The Dominicans consequently asked for the liberation of the Indians: 'for which reason it seems to us they should be taken out of the power of the Christians and given their freedom'; they state clearly that a return to their original primitive way of life is preferable to the exploitation to which they are being subjected. This for two reasons: first because, 'though they would gain nothing in their souls, they would at least gain life and the possibility of multiplying, which is less bad than losing everything'. This was a daring proposition which amounted to saying that the freedom and bodily health of infidels was of more importance than making them Christian slaves destined to die; or, as las Casas was to put it, better a live infidel Indian than a dead Christian one. The 'materialism' of such a view was clear to all, but with great spiritual freedom these friars felt more moved by the gospel and what they saw in the Indies than by the distinctions and hierarchies established by theologians.

The second reason is no less significant. The Dominicans wrote: 'Better that the Indians should remain in their lands such as they are, than that the name of Christ should be blasphemed as it is being blasphemed in the lands of the infidel'. Those who blasphemed the name of Christ were precisely those who exploited the Indians and—as the missionaries put it—rather than populating the Indies 'came to de-populate them'. It was impossible for the local commander to teach the Christian faith to those who were handed over to him, 'Because how can anyone teach the faith to the infidel when he himself does not know it, and worse still, does not practise it?'. Not practising it is worse than not knowing it, or, more precisely, it is the true not knowing it, because exploiting the poor is denying faith in Christ Jesus. The viewpoint of the poor and oppressed always brings us out of the realm of abstract principles to situate us inescapably on the hard terrain of practice, and of the gospel truth.[9]

The stance adopted by this daring group of Spanish Dominicans and the subsequent discussions gave rise to what has become known as the *debate on the Indies*. Its later development, in the thought of Vitoria, Domingo de Soto and others, was on more juridical and theological lines, in the mould of Thomas Aquinas, interpeting the facts in the light of the law of nations, not to mention natural law and its theological implications. Underlying the friars' protests is a clear affirmation of the basic equality of all human beings, which is why they put forward their defence of the Indians as the postulation of a natural and human right. But beyond this there is undoubtedly their perception of the Indians as poor and oppressed, as pre-eminently the neighbour to be loved. So, human rights certainly, but not in a liberal, formally egalitarian sense; rather on the lines of the *rights of the poor*. And within this, and most importantly, the poor seen not as isolated individuals, but formed into a people, an oppressed nation, a despised race condemned to death and destruction by the oppressor. There is not, as some would fear, any loss of universality in this view; it gains in true universality through its historic specificity and evangelical realism, the roots of all true prophecy.

Following this same train of thought, las Casas stressed the links between *gold* and *death*. What killed the Indians was the greed of the *conquistadores*, concerned only with 'acquiring monies'. This lust for gold was what took 'lives before their time'. Gold thus became the new lord, the adored idol paid in tribute of human sacrifice.

For Fray Bartolomé, too, the matter was not merely one of evil intentions: the logic of the new system imposed it. 'I am not saying,' he wrote perspicaciously to the Council of the Indies, 'that they desire to kill them directly, out of hatred they feel for them, but they seek to become rich and have an abundance of gold, which is their aim, through the labours and sweat of the afflicted and oppressed Indians, using them as means and dead instruments, from which there follows, of necessity, the deaths of all of them.' The death of the Indian was therefore a necessary consequence of the alienated labour system on which the new order was built, a social system designed to satisfy the interests and greed of the conquerors. The murderer of the poor is not really an individual impelled by evil instincts, but an oppressive social system based on the interest and gain of the conqueror, and on the accumulation of wealth in the hands of a few. (Thereby creating a situation of deep injustice contrary to the will of God.) Las Casas denounced the social order based on gold from the standpoint of faith, since, as he wrote, not without a fine sarcasm, 'Christ did do likewise, he did not come into the world to die for gold, but in order to suffer for men and to save them'.

Las Casas founded his defence of the Indians precisely on his love of Christ and desire to imitate him. The passion that drove him on was his love for the living Christ, flagellated, struck, crucified and put to death in the persons of the 'poor captives' of the Indies. Hence his conviction that loving Christ meant freeing the Indians and preventing 'their lives being taken before their time'. Once more, and this time identifying them with Christ, there is this sharp feeling for the poor, in their specific, material, temporal lives. In his theology we reach the ultimate truth: Christ calls from the life and death of the oppressed. So an exploitative régime imposed by 'those who call themselves Christians' is denounced and a call made to greater fidelity to the gospel.

This is not the view of the poor that emerges from the works of that great humanist Francisco de Vitoria. The standpoint from which he laid the foundations of international morality and law was that of progressist humanity, opening up trade and dealings between nations. Not that he was lacking a vision of the world entering on its modern era, nor capacity to theologise the new elements systematically, and certainly not in feeling for the equality of mankind; but he lacked direct contact with the situation of oppression of the Indian peoples and the evangelical demands that sprang from it. This is why, despite his energetic rejection of the motives generally adduced for making war and subjecting the Indians, he reintroduced their possibility under the form of hypotheses that would justify such wars in certain cases.

His position is more concerned with the progressive, modern wing of the conquering nations than with the Indian peoples. Las Casas and other missionaries opposed this; for them honest proclamation of the formal equality of all men was not enough; what they had experienced in the Indies led them to take another viewpoint, that of exploited humanity, the Indians, the poor in the gospel sense; in the final analysis, of the God of life.

They adopted this standpoint in the context of relations between Europe and what was later to become known as Latin America, but it is evidently valid for any oppressive, colonial régime in the world. And today, faced with what François Perroux has called 'the greed of nations', to which must be added the greed of the ruling sectors within each country, their attitude has lost none of its relevance to international morality.[10]

3. 'I DO NOT POSSESS TO EXPRESS MY LIFE, BUT MY DEATH'

The radicality of their standpoint prevents us from seeing the struggle for the liberation of the Indians in the sixteenth century as something belonging purely to its period or confined to its continent. On the contrary, the challenge from the poor and the oppressed has become stronger and more demanding in recent years. This is what the basic Christian communities, undoubtedly one of the most fruitful products of recent ecclesial experience in Latin America, are telling us with strength, imagination and prophecy.

The demands of the gospel are unchanging, and this makes them always new. They reject a world built on plunder and exploitation, because trampling on the most basic rights of the poor and oppressed is repudiating the Son of God who became one of them in history. Over the centuries, this has been one of the deepest mystical intuitions and one of the most inspiring sources of action for the Christian community in history. The ethic of being a disciple rests on this meeting with Christ in the poor. This is the great theme of Matthew's gospel, where the preaching of Jesus is presented as beginning with the promise of the kingdom to the poor (ch. 5) and ending with entry into it through a specific gesture towards the poor (ch. 25). The kingdom and the poor form an indissoluble unity.

The ethic of being a disciple is played out in the dialectic of grace and demand. The disciple is faced with the demand in time, in history; the community of disciples is the Church, of which it is therefore demanded that it be faithful to the practice of Jesus.[11] All this is bound up in and is a consequence of the gift of the kingdom, the basic gratuitous act which underlies all else. The behaviour of the disciple is judged on this basis, and Matthew tells us the criterion for this judgment: 'By their fruits you shall know them' (see ch. 7). These fruits, whose absence invalidates the exercise of any charism for the kingdom, (see Matt. 7; 1 Cor. 13), are what the Bible describes with the technical term 'works of mercy' or 'good works'. They are shown to be specific gestures towards the poor: giving food, drink, clothing. What Matthew specifically states—and this is what gives the criterion its definitive force—is that by carrying out these demands, by these 'good works' for the poor, we meet Christ himself. And this meeting is grace.

On their most elemental level, these works mean giving life, the life that we tend to call 'material', but which is in fact that human life defended so energetically by those sixteenth-century missionaries. This tells us that the kingdom of God has to do with food, health, clothing, drink: daily realities outside which we cannot perceive the specific and historical demands of the love of the Father, nor the grace of the fullness and abundance of life for which he sent his Son into the world.

The effort of the basic Christian communities, at the present juncture of history on the sub-continent of Latin America, is directed to this level of simple, basic intuitions, in the dialectic between grace and demand. And it seems clear that this dialectic can only be lived in the context of struggle against what destroys and assassinates the poor. To take one example: what is happening in El Salvador—the experience of which is with me as I write—poses the question in these terms.

The assassination of Mgr Romero is undoubtedly a landmark in the course of the Church of Latin America. In his Sunday homilies, his interventions with the great powers,[12] his support for popular front organisations, his constant call for a peace based on justice, Mgr Romero was risking his life. He received more than one threat of death. The murder of six priests was a close warning.[13] A month before his own death, he addressed the rulers of his country in these terms: 'Do not use violence to silence those of us who make these demands; do not go on killing those of us who are to achieve a just distribution of power and wealth in our country'. And he added, serenely and bravely: 'I speak in the first person, because this week I was warned that my name is on the list of those to be eliminated next week. But let it be understood that no one now can silence the voice of justice.'

He died—they killed him—for bearing witness to the living God (a constant theme in his preaching) in solidarity with the lives and the struggle for liberation of the poor and the oppressed. His faith brought him to this commitment; in this sense he was partial—in his commitment to the poor.[14] So not everything was on the same level for him in his overall human and Christian rejection of violence. On numerous occasions he declared that what was happening in El Salvador was caused chiefly by the age-old situation of plunder, of institutionalised injustice defended with repressive violence. This situation could not be accepted, and Mgr Romero did not accept it; it is against this background that the nature of his call for demanding, incarnate peace and love becomes clear. On 23 March he cried out in anguish and desperation to the army: 'In God's name and the name of this suffering nation whose cries rise to heaven every day, I beseech you, I implore you, I beg you, I order you: stop the repression'. The next day, his blood sealed the alliance he had made with his God, his people and his Church.

Martyrdom is the last act of life, a specific gesture toward the poor and so a meeting with the Lord. Contrary to what many people would have us believe, fighting against an oppressive system nourished on the blood of the poor is an option in favour of life. This is the martyr-bishop's message, and that of so many before and after him. With the poet César Vallejo, they can all say, 'I do not possess to express my life, but my death'. The spilt blood of the martyrs will always be opposed by those who claim, out of self-interest or intellectual conviction, that defence of the oppressed, as it has to be done in our present historical situation, involves a distortion or reduction of the gospel message. The witness of the martyrs will show up the real pettiness and alienation from the gospel of these power-ploys, accusations and jealousies. These witnesses to the faith and the resurrection of the Lord, the definitive victory of life over sin and injustice, prove that those who sow death will go away empty-handed, and that only the poor have their hands full of history and life.

Translated by Paul Burns

Notes

1. See the document *Towards a Church of Solidarity with the Poor*, published by the Commission for Participation in Development (CPID) of the World Council of Churches (Geneva 1979).

2. 'Dános nuestro pan de cada día' *Páginas* (Lima), Dec. 1979.

3. M. Vidal *El discernimiento ético* (Madrid 1980) pp. 69-87.

4. Medellín (1968) 'Peace'.

5. Let us not forget the example of Negro slavery and its trail of death. For a long time—and it is not quite over—this scandalous contempt for a human race was a daily fact accepted by a white Christian world which failed to see the perversity and sin inherent in racism. This is what black theology denounces today with such vigour.

6. Puebla condemns 'systematic or selective repression, with its accompaniments of delation, violation of privacy, extortionate fines, torture and exile' (42).

7. Puebla, 1209, based on a statement by John Paul II in his address to the conference.

8. Texts quoted on the following pages are taken from B. de las Casas *Historia de las Indias*, vols. I-II of *Obras escogidas* (Madrid 1957-8); letters and memoranda of the period reproduced in *Libro anual* (Mexico 1974).

9. What is at stake here is the manner in which faith is understood. *A propos* John 3:21 ('he who does what is true'), a text often quoted in this context, I. de la Potterie claims this is 'a biblical and Jewish expression' meaning 'to practise justice'. But then, going on to show that this meaning is 'the object of radical reinterpretation' in John's gospel, he states that the formula 'does not describe moral behaviour', i.e., 'acting in conformity with truth and inspired by it', but rather describes 'the access to faith', the 'way of faith', man's progressive adherence to Jesus' ('Faire la vérité: devise de l'orthopraxie ou invitation à la foi?', in *Le supplément* 118 (Sep. 1976) 279-293. The trouble is that his desire to criticise a certain kind of 'orthopraxis' seems to have forced his hand. Despite his efforts, it is difficult to see what John's 'radical reinterpretation' can consist of. Adherence to Jesus, living faith, is not recognition of an abstract truth, but imitation of a life and a praxis. See J. Mateos and J. Barreto *El Evangelio de Juan* (Madrid 1979).

10. On these subjects, see the recent book by V. Cosmao *Changer le monde: une tâche pour l'Eglise* (Paris 1979).

11. See H. Echegaray *La práctica de Jesús* (Lima 1980).

12. A few weeks before his death, Mgr Romero sent a letter to President Carter requesting, in the name of a slaughtered people, that the US government refrain from military intervention in his country, and demanding the prohibition of military aid to the army of El Salvador.

13. Since his death, one more priest has been killed.

14. See the commitment, sealed by tens of deaths, signed by eleven bishops on the tragic day of Mgr Romero's funeral, in *Páginas*, May 1980.

Enrique Dussel

Analysis of the Final Document of Puebla: The Relationship between Economics and Christian Ethics

1. CHRISTIAN ETHICS AND ECONOMY

IN THIS analysis of some aspects of the relationship between Christian ethics and economy in the Final Document of the Third General Conference of the Episcopate of Latin America held at Puebla de los Angeles in Mexico in February 1979, I propose to start with a brief clarification of the meaning I attribute to the two terms of the relationship: Christian ethics and economy.[1]

(a) Ethics

It is generally thought that ethics consists essentially of principles, norms, laws and values. But the *real* place of ethics is in *praxis* itself, and what is done is ethical not because it conforms to norms, or realises values, or produces virtues, but by reason of something that antedates these and is more important. *Praxis* refers to an action directed to another person (that other Greek term *poiesis*, by contrast, refers to actions directed to nature). Robinson Crusoe, alone on his island, could not carry out any *praxis*, but only productive actions (*poiesis*). Erotic praxis (an embrace), pedagogical praxis (a lesson), political praxis (a vote), religious praxis (adoration of the Absolute), are all positive acts. Praxis is the *place* of ethics. The ethical is an aspect of the working-out of interpersonal praxis. The ethical content of praxis is what lies beyond its specific content (the embrace, lesson, vote, prayer): the *way* in which I approach the other as other, a person as a person. Ethics is *how* I treat, manipulate, respect, use or serve . . . the other as such.

The question now is being able to decide *when* a praxis is ethically positive or good, or negative or perverse. Judgment *of* praxis, or *on* praxis, is not the essence of ethics, but a secondary, reflective, accidental moment in it. Classical thought laid down 'Do good' as a practical universal criterion. But this is too abstract (since every individual, system, etc., regards its own ends as 'good': even the aim of domination seems good to the dominator). Kant thought that: 'Take the person as an end and not as a means', was a

H
101

valid criterion. But a masochist can take his persecutor as an end without making the praxis good. It would seem that the *absolute* criterion (valid in *every* possible situation), which is at the same time specific and historical (it is always *this* someone, but at any moment can be *another*), is: 'Free the poor and oppressed'. This criterion, in every system and human relationship, challenges domination of man by man and works in favour of the dominated. This is an absolute criterion, at once the most critical and the most generous. The action of liberating the oppressed is the standard by which to judge the ethical goodness of all other actions. On the other hand, 'Dominate the other; achieve your ends by means of him', would seem to be an absolute criterion of evil and perversity. I hope we can take this as agreed, since explanations would be lengthy.[2]

(b) Christian Ethics

Christian praxis has much deeper motives than human goodness for fulfilling the absolute ethical criterion. Puebla refers to 'human beings who are capable of forging history in accordance with Jesus' "praxis" ' (*P* 178; *O* 279).[3] In effect, Christian ethical practice, or rather, Christian praxis, is what relates to the other *in the way* that Jesus Christ would have done in that specific historical situation. *Praxis* is defined by the fact that Jesus 'emptied himself to take the form of a servant' (Phil. 2:7, quoted in 3 instances in the Puebla Document, *O* 316, 744, 1141). Taking the part of the dominated in a system of slavery, being the poor, the servant, is the starting-point for Christian praxis, for Christian ethics. Being 'born in the likeness of men' (Phil. 2:7), dominated, poor, is the way to understand the overall meaning of the praxis of Jesus: 'The spirit of the Lord is upon me, because he has anointed me to preach good news to the *poor*' (Luke 4:18, quoting Isa. 61:1, the biblical text most often quoted in *O*: 327, 278-284, 1141, 1142, etc.). Subjective poverty not possessing in order to be free) and the struggle against objective poverty (that of the poor) distinguish Christian ethical praxis from the fetichistic praxis (*O* 493 ff) of those who build up the kingdom of this world. Of course there can be no poor people without rich people; the poor are produced by the sin of the rich, depriving them of the reward for their labour;[4] even the 'poor *in spirit*' (as opposed to the poor *by design*) cannot exist without the existence of the rich, the sinner, the dominator from whom the poor must accept humiliation, persecution, suffering in the name of their brethren: the wretched of the earth. If there were no rich people there would be no dominators, no sinners; we would be living not in historical time but in the time of the kingdom come, beyond the *paroisia*.

(c) Economy

As I have suggested recently,[5] economy, in its deepest anthropological and theological application deals with the *reality* of *practical* (erotic, pedagogical, political, religious) and *productive* (work transforming nature for human needs) relationships. The *practical* relationship on its own (the embrace) is abstract, momentary, not yet institutionalised, until it is measured by the factors (gift, house, etc.) that transform an erotic relationship into that of a couple. The economic relationship is that practical-productive relationship by which people relate to each other through the product of work, or by which things relate to each other by the people who produce them. So giving someone a present, or buying, or stealing, are all economic relationships. Worship of God is theological economy (by which the bread, or the body of the martyr, are offered to the absolute Other).

Ethics lies at the heart of economy in this sense, since it concerns, in the final analysis, the type or aspect of relationship established between two people as producers of certain products which are distributed, exchanged and consumed in different proportions, according to the type of practical relationship pre-established. When, for example, the Indo-Europeans with their iron weapons and horses conquered the agrarian civilisations of Mesopotamia and reduced them to slavery, this slavery became *real* when the new rulers (the class to which Aristotle belonged, for example) seized the products of the work of the ruled. Taking the fruits of the work of the slave is unjust, evil, not in itself (taking wheat and storing it in a barn), but because of the constitutive, pre-established domination of the master-slave relationship. The practical case (man-man relationship) becomes *real* in its economy; but the ethics of this economy proceeds from the constitutive practical relationship. If man dominates woman in society, the matrimonial home becomes the wife's prison and her work is exploited by her husband.

(*d*) Christian Ethics and Economy

The Christian praxis of liberating the oppressed, because the poor are Christ, mobilises economic relationships as such in their specific, historical and material being. 'I was hungry and you gave me food' (Matt. 35:25, quoted in *P* 111) is strictly economic in essence: it means simply giving someone some product of work. But giving food to the poor and the oppressed (who are hungry because they are poor), giving the dominated produce, is also to subvert the *system*, its *structures, mechanisms, institutions* (all terms used in the Puebla Document, as we shall see). Christian ethics, the praxis that imitates that of Christ, is situated on the plane of relationship between agents (between *those who* exchange, give, buy, steal, etc. 'something' with or to or from *someone*), and affirms or denies, changes or confirms this relationship in terms of the absolute criterion: 'Free the poor and oppressed'.

The Christian ethic is 'anti-fetichising' of the absolutisation of the practice of domination, and therefore atheistic of the idolatory of believing oneself to be God. Christian economy (or the type of relationship between people through the product of their work governed by Christian praxis) makes the Christian ethic *real*, makes it historical, specific, institutional, material. Not in the sense of cosmological or dogmatic materialism (*O* 313, 545-546), nor of practical or consumer materialism (*O* 314, etc.), but in that of sufficient, reconcilable-with-Christianity, *productive* materialism (the *material* product of work being an ineluctable reference by which finally to judge any historical action, since it is the sacramental or cultic, liturgical, meaning of nature as the theatre for the transforming action of work).

So the Christian economy clearly possesses a prophetic, denunciatory character (*O* 338, 1029, 1134, 1213, 1268, etc.). The so-called 'social teaching' of the Church can be taken as the sum total of denunciations made from defined positions at particular moments of history against excesses of capitalism (though not against its essence) and against the essence of socialism (as understood from the capitalist standpoint). But it is only Christian *economy*, which is neither a system nor a 'third way', that can provide the 'focus of intention' capable of judging a given economic system from the standpoint of Christian ethics: i.e., the relationship between agents through the products of their work. Or rather, it is only the productive or economic praxis of Christians that can, by analogy, intimate the economic praxis of Jesus: 'If any one would sue you and take your coat, let him have your cloak as well' (Matt. 5:40). This praxis, as one can see, shows that the logic of economic systems is not the absolute criterion of Christian economy, but that, on the contrary, Christian economic action always includes a critical, prophetic charge of Utopia, disorder, quest for a *juster* order of relationships between people through the medium of the product of their work. All historical economic or productive relationships must be judged by the relationship between people in the kingdom, where they will consist of the perfect economy, that is, its disappearance in the pure worship or liturgy offered by the Lamb to the Father.

2. THE CHRISTIAN ETHIC AT PUEBLA

In such a Conference as Puebla, different views leading to confrontations ('painful . . . tensions', *O* 102; 'tensions and conflicts', 246, etc.) were bound to arise.[6] What has been less noticed is the origin of such differences: different *real* situations or practical options (e.g., with regard to social class). I propose to take what seems to me the essence of the best of the Puebla Document first, and then I shall consider some other views.

(a) Mechanisms of social, structural and institutional Sin

All the participants at Puebla recognised sin as a *structural* reality (*O* 16, 30, *et al.*), as *institutionalised* violence (46, 1259), with its *mechanisms* (30, 70, etc.) which build up into a *system* ('sinful system' as in *O* 92 in particular). Sin understood in this way includes mere personal sinfulness (70, 72-75, 185 ff, 329, 330, etc.). But what is most important is that this historical or social sin is seen as a cause: which means that sin has an *effect*: 'In this anxiety and sorrow the Church sees a situation of social sinfulness . . . situation of inhuman poverty. . . . Analysing this situation more deeply, we discover that this poverty is not a passing phase. Instead it is the product of economic, social and political situations and structures, though there are also other causes for the state of misery' (*O* 28-30). Sin is related to poverty and indeed found to be its cause: a structural cause producing a structural effect. This is a Christian ethic which has overcome subjectivist individualism and progressed in historical, social objective and structural realism. Subjectivity is generated and co-implicated in the mechanism of institutional structures. At Puebla, one might say that the absolute *ego* seen as good or bad from an individual standpoint vanished, being judged instead by its roles, functions, historical behaviour and social, economic and political action.

(b) The Option for the Poor

No group, however subjectively opposed, could elude the basic commitment made to the poor and the oppressed. (This option is expressed tens of times, in phrases such as: 'Commitment to the poor and the oppressed', *O* 1147.) This 'clear and prophetic option, expressing preference for, and solidarity with, the poor' (*O* 1134) places Puebla in the basic line of Medellín, and makes it, compared with other episcopal documents of the Church, equally embarrassing to the wealthy Churches: 'Viewing it in the light of faith, we see the growing gap between rich and poor as a scandal and a contradiction to Christian existence . . . a situation of social sinfulness, all the more serious because it exists in countries that call themselves Catholic and are capable of changing the situation' (*O* 28).

Since there are no poor without the rich, and since poverty is structural, institutional and social, and situated on the plane of dispossession of one person of the fruit of his work to give it to another, this ethical option is not subjective, individualist or moralistic. It is an historical, social, objective, collective option: 'Sinfulness on the personal level . . . is always mirrored on the level of interpersonal relations . . . (producing) conflicts between individuals, groups, social classes and peoples' (*O* 328). So to opt for the poor is to opt for struggle on the level of groups, classes, peoples. It is to *enter into history in the reality of all history*. It is to apply the essence of Christianity globally.

(c) The Poor as a 'People'

More than this, the poor are understood as a collective subject, with the ability to organise themselves and with a consciousness of their own history, which is conflictive and liberating. The poor are not simply *this* individual, but the Amazon Indians, the American Negroes, the workers, the marginalised, the unemployed (*O* 31-39); they are the vast majority whose interests suffer for those of the few (47); those whose 'cry is rising to heaven . . . the cry of a suffering people who demand justice, freedom . . .' (87); the 'poor peoples' (130), with the reminder that, 'Jesus of Nazareth was born poor and lived as such among his people' (190). The poor are part of a *class*: 'The Church has intensified its commitment to the dispossessed segments' (here the word 'class' is avoided) '. . . This effort has given some the impression that the Church is disregarding the affluent classes' (147); but the concept of being part of a *people* is a richer one, and more historical, more real. And in Latin America, after nearly half a millenium of evangelisation, the poor are 'the People of God': 'The Church has turned its ear to this people, who are profoundly religious and who, for that very reason, place all their confidence in God' (93).

Of course the word 'people' should not be taken in the 'populist' sense (which includes the ruling classes in a project of national capitalism run by the bourgeoisie who then call themselves part of the 'people'); the category of 'people' should be seen in the context not so much of national as of basically social liberation: the liberation of the oppressed classes.

(d) The 'People's Church'

Because poverty should be seen not only as the individual situation of a person brought about by the circumstances of his life, but that of a people historically and structurally dispossessed, the Church's option for them cannot be merely the help given by the rich, the 'alms' given by the well-meaning, the moral, subjective decision of a few, but a commitment of the whole Church to this people: as a *people's* Church, taking on 'the form of a servant' (Phil. 2:7), like him who '*dwelt*[8] among us' (John 1:14). Puebla states that 'this view of the Church as a historical, socially structured People' means that it 'represents the broader, more universal, and better defined structure . . .' (*O* 261). Therefore, 'the problem of the "people's Church", the Church born of the People *or of the Holy Spirit*' (*P* 162; words in italics omitted in *O* 263) 'has various aspects. . . .' If it is interpreted as a Church that is trying to incarnate itself in the ranks of the common people on our continent, and that therefore arises out of their response in faith to the Lord' (*ibid.*), then the experience is valid. That is to say: the Christian ethical commitment has a *model* of the Church as its starting-point, a 'model' which exists in the prophetic *practices* of many Christians: of the great majority who are an oppressed people by birth and structure; of particular groups who opt for the people, in order to live with them, struggle on their behalf, take on their interests as part of the poor, oppressed and dispossessed. A missionary Church, an ethical light in Latin America, even in Nicaragua, in El Salvador, with Mgr Arnulfo Romero, martyr and hero of the people's Church.

3. ECONOMIC CRITICISM IN THE PUEBLA DOCUMENT

Ethical requirements turn these same prophetic Christian practices into denunciation of the 'economic *system*' (*O* 64, 67, etc.), on the level not of micro-economics (the company) but of macro-economics as structured by history. Here there is space to mention only a few aspects of this criticism.

(a) The Basis of Sin in economic Injustice

For Puebla, unlike earlier pronouncements, sin is not basically a matter of individual morality, particularly sexual morality, but situated on the level of history, structures, *economics*. In their 'Message to the Peoples of Latin America', the bishops stated: 'Because we believe that the re-examination and revision of people's religious and moral behaviour should be reflected in the political and economic processes of our countries, we invite all, regardless of class, to accept and take up the cause of the poor as if they were accepting and taking up their own cause, the cause of Christ himself.' 'Truly, I say to you, as you did it to one of the least of these my brethren, you did it to me' (Matt. 25:40). And again: 'There are many causes for this situation of injustice; but at the root of them all we find sin, both on the personal level and in structures themselves' (*O* 1258). And yet again: 'We want to point out some of the underlying roots of these phenomena. . . . The continuing operation of economic systems that do not regard the human being as the centre of society, and that are not carrying out the profound changes needed to move toward a just society. . . . Without trying to determine the technical character of these underlying roots, we ourselves see that at bottom there lies a mystery of sinfulness . . .' (*O* 63-70).

This means that sinfulness (the praxis of fetichistic domination) finds in the Puebla Document a massive condemnation as injustice on the level of the production, distribution, exchange and consumption of goods: goods of which the poor and oppressed are dispossessed by 'unjust social, political and economic structures' (*P* 920), by 'the mechanisms that generate this poverty' (*O* 1160). 'Thou shalt not steal', is seen by Puebla as referring first and foremost to 'Thou shalt not have strange gods before me', applied in its historical, structural, political sense.

(b) Developmentist and 'Third Way' Solutions

Puebla showed differing views on how to struggle against institutionalised, structural poverty and injustice. The developmentist option was firmly expressed: 'The significant economic progress that has been experienced by our continent *proves* (my italics) that it would be possible to root out extreme poverty and improve our people's quality of life' (*O* 21).

If it is considered that 'extreme poverty' can be rooted out, this still leaves us with poverty. The poor will be left at 'subsistence level'. What is being suggested is that it is possible to root out poverty within the dependent capitalist system; that therefore extreme poverty is not institutional, structural or intrinsic to the mechanisms of capitalism, but an eventual, casual product of it, one that can be avoided. This intra-capitalist optimism lies at the base of the developmentist theory, which is present in the Puebla Document not only in its economic passages, but in some Christological (a 'reforming' Christ) and ecclesiological ones (a denouncing Church, but from a *petty bourgeois* stance: criticising not the essence of capitalism but its excesses, like the *petit bourgeois*, who envies the capital of the *grand bourgeois*, not criticising capital as such, but only the fact that *others* have it, and in *large* amounts).

The 'third way' position (neither capitalist nor socialist: a Christian 'third way') was strongly represented in the Puebla Document, particularly thanks to the editorial process. There were four drafts, between each of which modifications (*modi*); could be introduced. If a Commission approved an anti-capitalist text, another group modified it with anti-socialist *modi* (this has happened at *O* 42-43, 45, 47-48, 54-58, 59-62, 79, 90-91, 92, 98, 437, and particularly 543-546, 550, etc.). So we are told: 'In the face of this situation, the Church chooses "to maintain its freedom with regard to the opposing systems, in order to *opt solely for the human being* (my italics). . . . It is not through violence, power-plays or political systems but through the truth about human beings that they will find their way to a better future (OAP: III 3)".' In this teaching Christianity is seen as providing its own historical model (perhaps Christian democracy, which today in El Salvador is supporting a *junta* which is destroying the people of the poor?); it is a model of a new Christendom which commits the Church to taking risks of a reformist capitalist nature, which blurs its image for evangelisaiton, and which unfortunately often coincides with the 'image of the Church as an ally of the powers of this world' (*O* 83). Furthermore, the decision to 'opt solely for the human being' immediately prompts the question: for the oppressor or the oppressed?—both are human beings. The section on the 'Social Teaching' of the Church (*O* 472-479) operates on about this level, and there is a culturalist vision diagnosing the need to support the transition from an 'agrarian culture' to a modern form of 'urban-industrial civilistion' (432), that fails to consider whether this transition can really be achieved with autonomy and without an increase in dependence and under-development.

(c) Structural Criticism of the economic system

But it is easy enough to discern another option in the Puebla Document. If it is true that it proposes 'to encourage the elaboration of viable alternatives in our evangelising activity that will be geared towards the Christian renovation of social structures' (*O* 1232), there is no hiding the fact that 'the ample hopes for development have come to nothing' (1260), and that this 'opens the way for alternative solutions to a consumer society' (1152). These alternatives, Utopian for some, the only way out for those sunk in the structural extreme poverty, tend to produce a more negative view of the present reality in opting radically for the poor: 'This option, demanding by the scandalous reality of economic imbalance in Latin America, should lead us to establish a dignified, fraternal way of life together as human beings and to construct a just and free society' (1154). By taking this position, the Christian is not putting forward another alternative model (just as Jesus did not put forward any precise political or economic solutions), such as Christian democracy, for example, but is on the other hand showing the incompatibility between Latin American dependent capitalism and the demands of the gospel, and opening the way to new alternatives, which will not be reformist but genuinely *new*: 'The free-market economy . . . is still the prevailing system on our continent. . . . It has increased the gap between the rich and the poor by giving priority to capital over labour' (47); 'A cold-hearted technocracy applies developmental models that extort a truly inhuman price from those who are poorest. And this is all the more unjust in so far as the price is not shared by all' (50). What the supporters of these models must now realise is that the Nicaraguan revolution, for example, is a sign that history is on the move and that the Lord of liberation can still allow David to conquer Goliath.

4. SOME ETHICO-ECONOMIC THEMES IN THE PUEBLA DOCUMENT

(a) Developmentist Industrialism

Some texts, as we have seen in 3 (*b*) above, tend towards modernisation *within* dependent capitalism (which they do not name, indeed whose existence they appear to be unaware of): 'We face an urgent situation. The shift from an agrarian to an urbanised, industrial society . . .' (460); 'an urban-industrial civilisation' (466) etc.

Although there is an awareness of 'the devastating effects of an uncontrolled process of industrialisation and a process of urbanisation that is taking on alarming proportions' (496), these are seen more as affecting the field of ecology, where causes and solutions are proposed. But there is a blindness in seeing capitalism's fetichistic need for expansion and profit as a cause of inadequate industrialisation. The capitalistic system is incapable of supplying the under-developed countries with an industry appropriate to their level of development and in accordance with the needs of the great majority of their people. The logic of capital means that industries are for export to the countries of the centre (exploiting the low wages paid in the countries of the periphery), or for the ruling classes of the poor countries (a minority who can acquire goods that show a profitable return). Both industrialisation and urbanisation are products of imperialist and dependent capitalism, but Puebla is silent on this point. This is intra-capitalist reformism.

(b) Economic Dependence

Yet there are texts in the Document clearly opposed to the developmentist option, which show the existence of structural dependence: 'There is the fact of economic, technological, political and cultural dependence; the presence of multinational conglomerates that often (or rather always?—*Author*) look after their own interests at the expense of the welfare of the country that welcomes them in' (*O* 66). There is frequent criticism of 'socio-political imbalance on the national and international levels' (1266), 'imbalance in international society' (1275). This shows that Puebla has a critical economic view which understands the international order as *one*, in which the riches of some are the cause of the poverty of others, bringing about 'the growing gap between rich and poor' (28).

Of course the struggle against dependence can be led by the bourgeoisie of a poor country setting up in competition with the bourgeoisie of the developed countries of the centre. This would be a 'populist' process of liberation (even if supported by the people, it is still capitalist). On the other hand, the struggle for liberation from dependence led by the popular classes is directed against capitalism itself, and directed to the formation of a post-capitalist society. Both positions find expression in the Puebla Document.

In any case, poverty as the fruit of sinfulness is seen as: 'exploitation caused by the organisational systems governing economics and international politics', which means that 'the underdevelopment of our hemisphere can grow worse and even become permanent' (1265).

(c) The Spread of the Multinationals

Dependence on capitalism of the centre is at present organised through the expansion of multinational corporations. 'In many cases the power of the multinational businesses overrides the exercise of sovereignty by nations and their complete control over their natural resources' (1264). This leads Puebla to proclaim, 'The right of each nation to defend and promote its own interests *vis-à-vis* multinational enterprises. On the international level there is now a need for a set of statutes that will regulate the activities of such enterprises' (1277). This means achieving 'a new international order with the human values of solidarity and justice' (1279).

(d) Militarism and dependent Capitalism

Since the 1960s in Latin America, pressure from the masses—accompanied and even inspired by the people's Church, with its heroes *and martyrs*—has become so strong that only a repressive State, which uses the army as its executive arm, can develop the model of dependent capitalism. The ideology of this repressive State has been named 'National Security'. At Puebla, condemnation of military régimes helped to power by North American influence and operating for the benefit of the multinationals and their dependent national bourgeoisie, coupled with demand for respect for the exercise of human rights, gained rapid acceptance from the vast majority (with the exception of some bishops from the southern tip of the continent, notably Argentina, where some bishops refused to agree with such a condemnation). So it is said that: 'the theory of National Security . . . enrols the individual in unlimited service to the alleged total war against . . . the threat of communism' (314). It is again named and condemned in 510, and in 547: 'In some countries of Latin America this doctrine justifies itself as the defender of the Christian civilisation of the West. It elaborates a repressive system, which is in line with its concept of "permanent war".' There is also, however (1247), an expression of hope in the evangelisation of the armed forces (and therefore of the effective holders of power in Latin America), rather than in that of the people of the poor.

(e) Defence of the economic rights of the Oppressed

Finally, we should note that Puebla declares in favour of defence of 'fundamental rights' (1268 ff) 'faced with the situation of sin'. These are defined as the right to life, to *work* (a basic right often forgotten, and which dependent capitalism, with its structural unemployment, cannot assure), to a home, to health, to development; the right of those emigrating from poverty for political reasons to shelter, refuge and amnesty, to freedom from torture, respect for the person and the right of free association. Puebla inveighs against the 'anxieties' forced on many people by 'systematic or selective repression . . . accompanied by accusations, violations of privacy, improper pressures, tortures and exile' (42).

Such processes are not brought about by psychological sadism, but by 'economic, social, and political *structures*' that produce poverty (30)—poverty and hunger that drive peoples to fight for their liberation.

Translated by Paul Burns

Notes

1. See my *De Medellín a Puebla (1968-1979)* (Mexico 1979); also my article 'Condiciones de la producción e interpretación del Documento de Puebla' *Servir* 81 (1979). On 'economy', see my article 'The Christian Art of the Oppressed in Latin America' *Concilium* 132 (February 1980) 40-52.

2. This question is the basic subject of my work *Etica filosófica latinoamericana* (latest vols. nos. IV and V, Bogotá 179-180), and the more popular *Ethic and Theology of Liberation* (1978).

3. The final document of the Puebla Conference as it emerged from the bishops is referred to as *P*, and the author quotes from this. It was then edited once more, mainly with the effect of breaking

down long paragraphs into several shorter ones, and published in Spanish in Bogotá by CELAM. This version is the one translated for the national Conference of Catholic Bishops in Washington, DC (published in the British Commonwealth by St Paul Publications and the Catholic Institute for International Relations), as the translation of the 'Official Conclusions . . .'. Since this is the only version likely to be available to English-speaking readers, references here are to this, denominated O (unless some words or meanings have been omitted or changes) (*Trans.*). The concordance between passages quoted in P and O is as follows:

P	O	P	O	P	O	P	O
8	16	50	90-91	234	338	905	1141
14	21-3	52	93	262	278-84	906	1142
17	28	58	98	263	385	911	1147
18	29	62	102	307	432	917	1152
19	30	73	127-130	312	437	919	1154
23	42-3	84	147-8	332	460	920	1156
25	46	101	185-6	338	466	925	1160
26	47-9	105	190-1	343	472	973	1213
27	50	111	198	364	493	981	1221
29	54-8	146	246	367	496	984	1224
30	59-62	160	261	379	507	993	1232
31	63	162	263	406	545-6	1008	1247
33	67	178	279	407	547-8	1019	1258
35	64	210	313	410	551	1021	1260
36	66	211	314	411	552	1025	1264
38	70	213	316	579	737	1026	1265
40	72-5	224	327	585	744	1028	1268
42	79	225	328	623	782	1035	1275-8
46	83	226	329	833	1029	1039	1279
49	85-6	227	330	897	1134		

4. See my article 'The Kingdom of God and the Poor' *International Review of Mission* 270 (April 1979) 115-130.

5. 'The Christian Art of the Oppressed . . .', the article cited in note 1.

6. Article in *Servir*, article cited in note 1 above, which claimes that 'this social situation has not ceased producing tensions within the Church'.

7. There is even a dismissive reference to those who 'presume to justify their position with a subjective profession of Christian faith' (O 49).

8. 'Dwelt', or 'pitched his tent', from Heb. *skene, sekinah* in the OT (Exod. 33:7).

Apologies for so many references to my own works, which has been done in the interests of brevity.

Contributors

HANNS ABELE, born in Vienna in 1941, studied law at Vienna University and took his doctorate in that subject in 1963. After practising law he became in 1964 a university assistant at the Institute for Economic Sciences and studied political sciences and mathematics. In 1972 he took his *Habilitation* in political economy, and the following year was appointed to a professorship at Fribourg University. In 1977 he was appointed professor of political economy at the Economic University of Vienna. He has spent periods of study in Oxford and New York. His publications include: 'Über geldwirtshaftliche Wachstumsmodelle' *Zeitschrift für Nationalökonomie* 31 (1971); 'Towards a Neo-Austrian Theory of Exchange' *Equilibrium and Disequilibrium in Economic Theory* ed. G. Schwödiauer (Dordrecht 1977) pp. 204-212; 'Vom Glück und Unglück des Wohlstands und der Wirtschaftskrise' *La recherche du bonheur/Die Suche nach dem Glück* (Fribourg 1978) pp. 70-84; and 'Zur politischen Ökonomik des Nord-Süd-Dialogs und der Position der Kirche' *Unterwegs zur Einheit: Festschrift für Heinrich Stirnimann* eds. J. Brantschen and P. Selvatico (Fribourg 1980) pp. 135-154.

MARIE-DOMINIQUE CHENU O.P. was born in 1895 and was at one time Rector of the Dominican Faculty at Le Saulchoir, near Paris, and professor in the Faculty of Theology, Paris. He taught the history of theology in the middle ages in its sociological context and used the same method in order to gain a pastoral understanding of the Church today. He was a private counsellor at Vatican II. His publications include: *La Théologie comme science au XIII siècle* (1943); *Introduction à l'etude de St Thomas d'Aquin* (1950); *La Théologie au XII siècle* (1957); *Pour une théologie de travail* (1955); *L'Evangile dans le temps* (1964); *Peuple de Dieu dans le monde* (1966); *La Doctrine sociale de l'Eglise comme idéologie* (1979).

VINCENT COSMAO O.P. was born in Britanny in 1923. In the 1950s he served as a chaplain in the Universities of Lyons and Dakar, and from 1959-65 he was the Superior of the Fraternité Saint-Dominique in Dakar. P. Lebret appointed him assistant-director of IRFED, a post he held from 1966 until 1972, when he founded the Centre Lebret: Foi et Développement in Paris. His articles and books include *Changer le mond, une tâche pour l'Eglise* (Paris 1979) and he writes for *La Croix* on the relationship of Christianity and the developing countries. He lectures at the Institut Catholique de Paris.

ENRIQUE DUSSEL was born in 1934 in Argentina, and holds a doctorate in philosophy and history from the Sorbonne. He is at present teaching at the Autonomous University of Mexico. He is President of the Commission of Studies on the Church in Latin America (CEHILA), and has taken part in meetings for Ecumenical Dialogue of

Third World theologians in Dar-es-Salaam, Accra, Sri-Lanka and São Paulo. Of his many important works, those recently translated into English are: *History of the Church in Latin America* (Grand Rapids 1980) and *Ethic and Theology of Liberation* (New York 1978).

GEORGES ENDERLE was born at St Gallen, Switzerland, in 1943. He studied philosophy in München-Pullach and theology in Lyon-Fourvière. Since 1970 he has dedicated himself to the study of development problems and has made study tours in India, Peru, etc. Since 1973 he has studied economic sciences in Fribourg, Switzerland, where he is working on a doctoral thesis on the distribution of income and property in Switzerland.

GUSTAVO GUTIÉRREZ was born in Peru in 1928, and studied medicine before changing to philosophy and theology. He was ordained in 1959, and is professor of theology at the Catholic University of Lima. Now an educational director of *Concilium*, he co-edited the issue (96, June 1974) that first dealt with the theology of liberation, and his best-known work, *A Theology of Liberation* (New York and London 1973), has done more than any other to bring this to the attention of the English-speaking world. Most recently, he has contributed to *Frontiers of Theology in Latin America*, ed. R. Gibellini (New York 1979; London 1980).

SIRO LOMBARDINI was born in 1924. He was professor at the University of Milan between 1951-1963 and since 1963 he has been professor of politics, economics and finance at the University of Turin. He has also not only been visiting professor at such universities as Cambridge, Harvard and Leningrad, but been involved in active politics; he has, for instance, been a member of the Concilio nazionale della Programmazione between 1963-1976 and minister for state participation in the first ministry of premier Cossiga from July 1979 to August 1980.

JOHN LUCAL S.J. is currently the General Secretary of the joint Committee on Society, Development and Peace, of the Holy See and the World Council of Churches (SODEPAX), which has its offices in the Ecumenical Centre in Geneva, Switzerland. In this position he has come into contact with the work of numerous Church-related donor agencies, both Catholic and Protestant. Fr Lucal was born near Chicago, Illinois, U.S.A., and studied political science at Harvard and Georgetown, entering the Society of Jesus in 1951, and later taught for two years in Ethiopia. He earned the degrees of S.T.L. in theology and M.A. in philosophy, and did doctoral studies in international relations at Columbia University in New York, where he also served as an assistant editor of the Jesuit weekly, *America*. Before coming to Geneva, he was the adviser to the Permanent Mission of the Holy See at the United Nations in New York, primarily on disarmament and political affairs. He has published articles in various journals and now edits *Church Alert*, the SODEPAX Bulletin.

AMBROS LÜTHI was born in the canton of Solothurn, Switzerland, in 1938. He teaches mathematics and biology. He is a systems analyst for a computer organisation and an international expert on systems engineering with Third World connections which has given him an interest in development politics. He studied economic sciences in Fribourg, Switzerland, and wrote a thesis on the measurement of economic inequality. He is the author of a 'manifesto on behalf of freedom from domination' soon to appear in Basle.

ROGER RIDDELL works as an economist for the Catholic Institute for International

Relations in London. In 1977 he completed his postgraduate studies on Third World development at the Institute of Development Studies, Sussex, England. He has spent many years working in Zimbabwe, where he graduated from the national university in economics. He has published a number of books, monographs and articles on development issues in contemporary Zimbabwe and on the Church in Zimbabwe as well as studies on South Africa, and since this article was sent to the language editors, he has been appointed Chairman of a National Commission to investigate incomes, prices and workers' conditions in Zimbabwe by the Prime Minister, Mr Robert Mugabe. His published works include: *The Land Problem in Rhodesia: Alternatives for the Future* (CIIR, London and Mambo Press, Zimbabwe) and 'The Liberation of Theology and the Rhodesian Church' *The Month*, (May 1977).

HANS SCHÖPFER, born in 1940 at Schüpfheim, Switzerland, took his doctorate of theology in Rome after studying theology, sociology and psychology at several European universities. He has spent several years doing pastoral work in Latin America and has followed this by regular visits for study in that continent. He is lecturer in missiology at the University of Fribourg, Switzerland and works for missionary organisations in that country and as an expert on aid programmes for international co-operation. His publications include a study of liberation theology (*Lateinamerikanische Befreiungstheologie* 1977), and he has edited a volume of studies and documentation on the meeting of the Latin American bishops' conference held at Puebla, Mexico, in 1979 (*Kontinent der Hoffnung. Beiträge und Berichte zu Puebla* 1979).

DIETER SENGHAAS studied at Tübingen, Amherst, Ann Arbor and Frankfurt and, after spending two years between 1968-1970 at Harvard University, he directed research between 1971-1978 at the Hesse Foundation for peace and conflict studies. He held the chair of international politics at the University of Frankfurt between 1972-1978 and since 1978 he has been professor of social sciences at the University of Bremen, specialising in development research. He is a member of numerous national and international organisations for the promotion of social scientific research and has edited many books and written widely in scientific journals. His publications include: *Aggressivität und kollektive Gewalt* (Stuttgart 1972); *Rüstung und Militarismus* (Frankfurt 1972); *Gewalt-Konflikt-Frieden* (Hamburg 1974); *Weltwirtschaftsordnung und Entwicklungspolitik* (Frankfurt 1978); *Abschreckung und Frieden* (Frankfurt 1980).

PAUL STEIDL-MEIER S.J. is a member of the faculty of social sciences of the Pontifical Gregorian University, Rome. His training includes a Ph.D. from Stanford University in development economics (for which the dissertation was on modern Chinese agriculture) and a Th.M. from Harvard Divinity School in social ethics. Recent research has led to a forthcoming book, *Hunger and Injustice: Structural Problems in the World Food System*. A copious bibliography is included in this book.

PIETER VERLOREN VAN THEMAAT was born in Rotterdam in 1916. He gained a law degree in Leiden in 1946 and worked in the Dutch Ministry of Economic Affairs, 1945-1958. In 1958 he joined the EEC Commission as Director-General in charge of monitoring cartel agreements and misuse of economic power by business, and of supervising the States' support measures, tax problems and the harmonisation of national legislation. Since 1967 he has been professor of national and international economic law at the State University of Utrecht. His main publications include: *Economic Law of the Member States of the European Communities in an economic and monetary union* (Brussels 1973); *Rechtsgrondslagen van een nieuwe internationale economische ordre* (The Hague/Alphen a.d. Rijn 1979); in co-operation with P. J. G. Kapteyn *Inleiding tot het recht van de Europese Gemeenschappen* 3rd impr. (Deventer 1980).

JOHN PHILIP WOGAMAN has been professor of christian social ethics at Wesley Theological Seminary, Washington D.C., U.S.A., for the past 14 years and, since 1972, he has also served as Dean of that institution. Previously he taught for five years at the University of the Pacific in California. An ordained minister of the United Methodist Church, he earned the Ph.D. degree in social ethics at Boston University. He is a past president of the American Society of Christian Ethics. He has served on a number of ecumenical councils and committees, including active leadership in the Washington Theological Consortium since its founding. He is author of *Christians and the Great Economic Debate* (London 1977) (U.S. title *The Great Economic Debate: An Ethical Analysis* (Philadelphia)); *A Christian Method of Moral Judgment* (London and Philadelphia 1976, 1977); *Quality of Life in a Global Society* (New York 1978, with Paul McCleary); *The Population Crisis and Moral Responsibility* (edited, Washington, D.C. 1973); *Guaranteed Annual Income: The Moral Issues* (New York and Nashville, Tenn. 1968); and other books and articles.